The Book of JOB

The Book of
JOB

RICARDO GRAHAM

Pacific Press®
Publishing Association
Nampa, Idaho | Oshawa, Ontario, Canada
www.pacificpress.com

You can obtain additional copies of this book by calling toll-free 1-800-765-6955 or by visiting http://www.adventistbookcenter.com.

Library of Congress Cataloging-in-Publication Data
Names: Graham, Ricardo, 1950-
Title: The book of Job / Ricardo Graham.
Description: Nampa, Idaho : Pacific Press Publishing Association, 2016.
Identifiers: LCCN 2015045663 | ISBN 9780816360994 (pbk.)
Subjects: LCSH: Bibile. Job—Criticism, interpretation, etc.
Classification: LCC BS1415.52 .G57 2016 | DDC 223/.106—dc23 LC record available at http://lccn.loc.gov/2015045663

ISBN 978-0-8163-6099-4

May 2016

Dedication

First, I dedicate this book to the True Author,
Jesus Christ the Righteous.

And to my loving wife, Audrey Weir-Graham, who has
encouraged my speaking and writing ministry throughout our
marriage.

To our children, Jessica and Jonathan, who have blessed me
with their penetrating and critical thinking along the way.

And to my friend Pastor Byron K. Hill Sr., my true friend
who "bugged" me to write to God's glory.

Contents

The Perennial Question

Despite all the popular propaganda to the contrary, Christians have very logical and rational reasons to believe in God. Though assured by some of the "best and brightest" that the evolutionary concepts of "natural selection" and "random mutation" can explain the complexity, wonder, and beauty of life—many people don't buy it and logically so. And despite the latest "scientific" pronouncements that the universe arose from "nothing," most people find the idea of an eternally existing God, as opposed to "nothing," the more logically satisfying explanation for Creation.

And yet, even with logic and reason firmly on our side, there's still the ever-present problem of evil. And thus the perennial question: *If God exists and is so good, so loving, and so powerful, why so much suffering?*

Hence, this quarter's study: the book of Job. How fascinating that Job, which deals with the perennial question, was one of the first books of the Bible written. God gave us, early on, *some* answers to the most difficult of all issues.

Some answers, but not all. Probably no one book of the Bible could answer them all; even the Bible as a whole doesn't. Nevertheless, Job pulls back a veil and reveals to the reader the existence of a reality beyond what our senses, even those aided by scientific devices, could show us. It takes us to a realm that while far removed from us in one sense is incredibly close in another. The book of Job shows us what so much of the rest of the Bible does, too: the natural and supernatural are inseparably linked. Job is a portrayed drama of the principle and warning that Paul expressed ages later: "For we do not wrestle against flesh and blood, but against principalities, against powers, against the rulers of the darkness of this age, against spiritual hosts of wickedness in the heavenly places" (Ephesians. 6:12, NKJV).

Though mostly about one man, the book of Job is the story of us all, in that we all suffer in ways that often seem to make no sense. And even the story of the four men who come to him reflects our situation, too; for who among us hasn't tried to come to grips with the sufferings of others?

Yet, we'd miss a crucial point about the book of Job if we limited it only to suffering humanity's attempts to understand suffering humanity. The story appears in a context, that of the great controversy between Christ and Satan, that is portrayed here in the most literal of terms. And that's because it's the most literal of battles, one that began in heaven and is being played out here in the hearts, minds, and bodies of every human being.

This quarter's studies look at the story of Job—both close up, in the immediate drama of the narrative, and from a distance, in that we know not only how the book ends but also the bigger background in which it unfolds. As readers, then, with the knowledge not only of the book of Job but of the whole Bible, one crucial issue for us is to try and pull it all together. We try to understand, as much as possible, not only why we live in a world of evil but also, more important, how we are to live in such a world.

Of course, even after we study Job, even in the context of the rest of the Bible, the perennial question remains. We are assured, though, of the perennial answer: Jesus Christ, in whom "we have redemption through His blood" (Ephesians 1:7, NKJV)—the One through whom all answers come.

Clifford R. Goldstein is the editor of the Adult Bible Study Guide. *He has been at the General Conference since 1984.*

CHAPTER 1

Beginnings and Endings

In his book, *The 7 Habits of Highly Effective People,* first published in 1989, the late author Stephen R. Covey lays out established principles that business people have used to succeed in their endeavors. These principles are useful in every area of life.

Covey's habit number 2 suggests that it is best to begin with the end in mind. In other words, it is advisable to envision the expected or desired outcomes and to move to actualize that vision. And so, we start our study of the book of Job at the end of his life.

If we were in complete control of planning our physical longevity, we wouldn't include illness, disease, and death in our plans. Since we are not capable of this, we must face death as Job did.

The Bible does not record God's response to Job's "Why?" questions. The deaths of all ten of his children, the theft and destruction of his property, and the loss of his health—no direct explanation to Job is recorded. This unknown must have intensified Job's suffering.

In fact, Job's story concludes, "So Job died, being old and full of days" (Job 42:17, KJV); almost as if the writer infers that the consolation for his suffering and eventual death was having a long life. Though he was richer and wiser than before, he still died.

As we study the Word of God, we do not come to a conclusion

based on one or two texts, but we try to examine all the textual information on a subject in their proper contexts before arriving at a conclusion (see Isaiah 28:13).

The Bible certainly is not a fairy tale that ends with, "They all lived happily ever after," and all the personalities recorded in the Bible died—with the exception of Enoch and Elijah, both of whom were translated to heaven. Even Jesus tasted death, exiting his "borrowed" grave to life everlasting.

While an obvious, desired goal of humanity is to secure happiness, the Bible doesn't gloss over the tragedies in life. All of our lives lived between Eden and heaven and the renewed Earth are filled with temptations, trials, trouble, and tribulations, and none of us will escape death.

As Benjamin Franklin said, "In this world nothing can be said to be certain, except death and taxes." The certainty in this life is that we will all end up dead.

This life is filled with a full range of unhappy endings, from the trivial to the life-changing, challenges surround us. Our favorite sports team loses. Our children don't do well in school; they hang out with the wrong crowd; they choose marriages that all too often end in divorce. Despite being vegetarians and vegans, many of us contract disease; illness stalks us like a hungry lion chasing her prey on the African plains.

The fact that life is full of unhappy endings should not surprise us. The Bible tells us that our enemy seeks to devour us: "Be alert and of sober mind. Your enemy the devil prowls around like a roaring lion looking for someone to devour" (1 Peter 5:8).

Job's end teaches us to be aware of that fact and to deal with life knowing that we are, short of the Second Coming, going to die.

The story of Job demonstrates that the way we face life is the way we will face death. By examining how Job lived his life at the beginning, we are better able to understand how he faced the end.

And what Job didn't fully know is that the end of his story is not the end of *the* story. It is not the final ending. Someone has said that the word *history* can be written as *His story*; it is the story of God's interaction and intervention in a world gone wrong.

And we can know that while Job suffered loss, pain, and

mental anguish, God was with him all the way through to the end. In the same way, He is also with us.

Not only that, but Job arrives at a much deeper understanding of the ways of God, far beyond the surface knowledge that he and his three friends had at the beginning of the narrative. All four of them misunderstood and misrepresented God.

His friends worked from the false assumption that Job's calamities were caused by some secret, unconfessed sin. Job, in response, presented himself as altogether righteous. Neither position was correct.

In response to God's question: "Who is this that obscures my plans without knowledge?" Job says, "Surely I spoke of things I did not understand, things too wonderful for me to know" (Job 42:3, 4). God's self-revelation through a series of questions recorded in chapters 38–41 challenges Job's limited understanding of the Divine.

Job's previous knowledge was limited and inconclusive and thus, wrong. He confesses his limited understanding of God and shares where he received his misshapen ideas: "My ears had heard of you but now my eyes have seen you" (Job 42:5).

Job confesses that his previous knowledge of God was based on what he had heard from others; in other words, it was second-hand or hearsay at best. His theological training, as it were, was based fully on the witness of others.

What others have experienced with God is important, but it is still not as important as what we can learn from God in our personal experience with the Creator, Sustainer, and Redeemer.

However, at the end of the story, Job reveals he has passed through an experience, hearing and "seeing" God for Himself. (This is not a declaration of a literal or visionary sighting of God.) His suffering and the false accusation of his friends had led him to question God, and finally, God spoke to him directly.

"In this statement Job reveals the transition from a religious experience shaped by tradition to an experience based on personal communion with God."[1]

"Job's religious experience is no longer second-hand; he has met God personally, and this makes all his sufferings worthwhile."[2]

At the end of his experience and after listening to God's questioning, Job states he has seen God for himself. And after this deep experience of suffering and listening to his three friends and finally hearing God ask questions of him, Job rightly repents and assumes the deep self-humiliation position customary for his times of sitting in dust and ashes (Job 42:6).

Another aspect of Job's tale is the highly significant practice of intercessory prayer found in verse 10. The Bible connects Job's restoration to his praying for his three friends, Eliphaz the Temanite, Bildad the Shuhite, and Zophar the Naamathite. This concept is not to be glossed over.

The emphasis on intercessory prayer is found throughout Scripture. Take the example of the prophet Daniel. One commentary states the following:

> A wonderful model of intercessory prayer is found in Daniel 9. It has all the elements of true intercessory prayer. It is in response to the Word (v. 2); characterized by fervency (v. 3) and self-denial (v. 4); identified unselfishly with God's people (v. 5); strengthened by confession (v. 5-15); dependent on God's character (vv. 4, 7, 9, 15); and has as its goal God's glory (vv. 16-19). Like Daniel, Christians are to come to God on behalf of others in a heartbroken and repentant attitude, recognizing their own unworthiness and with a sense of self-denial. Daniel does not say, "I have a right to demand this out of You, God, because I am one of your special, chosen intercessors." He says, "I'm a sinner," and, in effect, "I do not have a right to demand anything." True intercessory prayer seeks not only to know God's will and see it fulfilled, but to see it fulfilled whether or not it benefits us and regardless of what it costs us. True intercessory prayer seeks God's glory, not our own.[3]

Jesus provided the ultimate example of intercessory prayer while dying on the cross, saying, " 'Father, forgive them, for they do not know what they are doing.' And they divided up his clothes by casting lots" (Luke 23:34). What a privilege to have someone pray for us, and what a responsibility to tell someone that we will pray for them!

To pray *for* someone is altogether different from praying *about* someone. It is a positive intercession on behalf of someone else; speaking to God on behalf of others should be a delightsome experience for all Christians.

While it is not explicitly stated, Job understood that he was to pray a prayer of blessing for his mistaken friends. The great and gracious God instructs us to pray for people, not just about them.

Not only did Jesus demonstrate this deep forgiveness by interceding for His executioners at the end of His ministry, He taught this as heaven's expectation in His sermon on the mount: "But I say unto you, Love your enemies, bless them that curse you, do good to them that hate you, and pray for them which despitefully use you, and persecute you" (Matthew 5:44, KJV).

Job's praying for his offending friends foreshadowed Christ's teaching, which was a revelation of God's great merciful and forgiving heart.

Jesus further stipulated that our forgiveness should be limitless when Peter asked Him how many times should he (or we) forgive someone who sins against him (or us), "Then Peter came and said to Him, 'Lord, how often shall my brother sin against me and I forgive him? Up to seven times?' Jesus said to him, 'I do not say to you, up to seven times, but up to seventy times seven' " (Matthew 18:21, 22, NASB).

What Jesus is indicating and what is presented in an embryonic form in the book of Job is that forgiveness is unlimited; forgiveness is not a matter of mathematics or legal regulations, but an attitude.[4] In fact, Ellen White writes that "nothing can justify an unforgiving spirit."[5]

One further truth is revealed here: Our forgiveness is inextricably bound to the forgiveness we grant to those who offend us. "For if you forgive others for their transgressions, your heavenly Father will also forgive you. But if you do not forgive others, then your Father will not forgive your transgressions" (Matthew 6:14, 15, NASB).

Can it be any plainer than that?

Job understood. And it was not until after he prayed for his friends that he was restored. While this was Job's experience, it is not to be understood that material prosperity and health will automatically come when we are involved in intercessory prayer. We do know, however, that the preponderance of the biblical information is that God is pleased when we pray for each other (see James 5:16 and 1 John 5:16).

The Bible does not specifically state that Job was healed of his ailments, but the context of chapter 42 points in that direction. His restoration must have been complete. And while he suffered with the company of his three miserable comforters, at the end, his siblings and many acquaintances surround him, rejoicing in his restoration.

The question may legitimately be asked, "Where were they when he was down-and-out?" Perhaps they too, along with Job's friends, believed that Job was getting his just reward, and they shunned the apparently guilty man. Now that he is healthy, wealthy, and whole, they are back at his side rejoicing. People can be fickle. Perhaps that is one motivating factor behind the psalmist writing, "Do not put your trust in princes, in human beings, who cannot save" (Psalm 146:3).

The same people who presumably enjoyed the largesse of Job when he was on top of the world abandoned him when he was sick and going through the depths of despair. But now that his fortunes are reversed, they are back in the fold again. Now that the trial is over, the trouble is gone, and the tribulations have ceased; they come to comfort him and bring him gold and silver (Job 42:11).

Contrast that with Jesus' triumphal entry into Jerusalem (Matthew 21:1–11). The entire city cried out "Hosanna to the Son of David! Blessed is He who comes in the name of the Lord! Hosanna in the highest!" (verse 9, NKJV). But when Jesus was brought before Pontius Pilate, the governor, the people cried out, "Crucify him!" (Matthew 27:22). Undoubtedly, there were those in the crowd who had witnessed Jesus' miraculous healings of the blind, crippled, and diseased. Joyfully welcoming Him during

His earlier entry into Jerusalem, they later turned against Him. In the end, like Job's trials, Jesus' trials from Gethsemane to the grave ended better than they started.

Job is blessed with more livestock and another set of sons and daughters in the same number as he had at the beginning: seven sons and three daughters. Interestingly enough, the daughters are named in verse 14, while the son's names are not mentioned: Jemimah, which means "handsome as the day;" Keziah, which means "a spice of fragrance;" and Keren-Happuch, which means "the horn of color" or "the colorful ray."

It is specifically mentioned that Job gave an inheritance to the daughters as well as to his sons, "an unusual favor in the East to daughters, who, in the Jewish law, only inherited, if there were no sons (Nu 27:8), a proof of wealth and unanimity."[6] And Job, who during his trial deplored his birth, lived an additional 140 years. Amazing, isn't it?

God promises that our end will be better than our beginning if we build our lives on the foundation that He has laid, Jesus Christ the Righteous Redeemer, about whom, in the midst of his despair, Job in faith confidently stated,

> "I know that my redeemer lives,
>   and that in the end he will stand on the earth.
> And after my skin has been destroyed,
>   yet in my flesh I will see God;
> I myself will see him
>   with my own eyes—I, and not another.
> How my heart yearns within me!" (Job 19:25–27).

So what can we learn from the last chapter of Job's book? There are many things that happen during our lives that we will not ever have a full and total understanding of. Even though we all go through trials and periods of difficulty, God is there on our side, and He will eventually reveal Himself.

While good-intentioned friends may try to comfort us in our sorrows, the ultimate source of comfort can be found in God alone. As we maintain our faith, it will be rewarded. Perhaps not as demonstrably as was Job's, but it will be rewarded, nonetheless. With God, our end will be better than our beginning.

If we begin with the end in mind and keep the preferred end in sight, we will inhabit a world and live a life altogether unlike anything we could ever imagine.

> Then I saw "a new heaven and a new earth," for the first heaven and the first earth had passed away, and there was no longer any sea. I saw the Holy City, the New Jerusalem, coming down out of heaven from God, prepared as a bride beautifully dressed for her husband. And I heard a loud voice from the throne saying, "Look! God's dwelling place is now among the people, and he will dwell with them. They will be His people, and God Himself will be with them and be their God. He will wipe every tear from their eyes. There will be no more death or mourning or crying or pain, for the old order of things has passed away" (Revelation 21:1–4).

This is the end God has in mind for us—an end that will glorify Him and Him alone—not that we could earn it by our faith but because of God's mercy and grace. Let's plan now to be there in the Earth made new, to see the end of this world transformed into a new beginning.

---

1. Francis D. Nichol, ed., *The Seventh-day Adventist Bible Commentary*, 2nd ed., vol. 3 (Washington, D.C.: Review and Herald®,1977), 610.

2. W. W. Wiersbe, Job 38:1–42:6 in *Wiersbe's Expository Outlines on the Old Testament* (Wheaton, Ill.: Victor Books, 1993).

3. "What Is Intercessory Prayer?" gotQuestions?org, http://www.gotquestions.org /intercessory-prayer.html#ixzz3clHjUy4b.

4. Francis D. Nichol, ed., *The Seventh-day Adventist Bible Commentary*, 2nd ed., vol. 5 (Washington, D.C.: Review and Herald®, 1980), 449.

5. Ellen G. White, *Christ's Object Lessons* (Mountain View, Calif.: Pacific Press®, 1900), 251.

6. "Job 42," *Jamieson-Fausset-Brown Bible Commentary*, Bible Hub, http://bible hub.com/commentaries/jfb/job/42.htm.

CHAPTER 2

The Great Controversy in Job

If we had never read the story of Job before, perhaps we would be pleasantly surprised at the opening of this epic tale. Immediately, he is commended for possessing four sterling characteristics: he is blameless, upright, God-fearing, and a person who shuns, or avoids, evil. To some, this may be the most astonishing statement in the book of Job. "In the land of Uz there lived a man whose name was Job. This man was blameless and upright; he feared God and shunned evil" (Job 1:1).

Reading further we find that he is a father of seven sons and three daughters. So far, so good. To top this all off, he is wealthy—not rich, but wealthy—and proclaimed to be the greatest man in the east. Wow! Religious, wealthy, and famous—what a trifecta!

As a religious man, he provided worship for his adult children after their feast days. He took personal parental responsibility for his adult offspring, just in case they had forgotten or cursed God. The Bible states Job did this with regularity. Our admiration of this man grows by leaps and bounds. The Bible paints the picture of a mature, serious, highly successful businessman. He was a husband and a father who trusted God.

We achieve this state of blamelessness, as it were, by "leaning on the everlasting arms"[1] of Jesus. It is an accomplishment that is directed by God the Holy Spirit as we yield to His presence in our lives.

I believe that Job was blameless in his relationships. We all live in relationship to each other, God, and to our communities. To be sure, there are "hermits" and other groups and individuals who may seek to stay away from other people, but no one can escape the view or the presence of God.[2]

Job's experience speaks universally. In principle, anything that we can experience today has already happened, because, as Solomon the wise man said, "There is nothing new under the sun" (Ecclesiastes 1:9).

The details of our individual experiences may differ, but the commonality is that we all, at some point in time, are tested, tried, and tempted. While it may not be as severe as Job's experience, we will all undergo some level of trouble.

It is clear, however, due to the pronouncement and articulation of God Himself (Job 1:8), that it is possible—despite all hellish opposition—to live a life pleasing to God at any time, in any society, under any political system. Remember what Jesus said, "With man this is impossible, but not with God; all things are possible with God" (Mark 10:27).

As the narrative continues, we assume that Job is living his life, minding his own business, when suddenly, unbeknownst to him, he becomes the subject of a dialogue between God and a fallen being, the angel previously known as Lucifer, now Satan.

There is a backstory, as they say, to every historical record of how things come to be, so it behooves the reader to pause in the current narrative and take a look at the history that is not provided in the book of Job regarding this aspect of the tale.

Certain questions have been asked for centuries about the origin and continuation of evil in this world. Who created the devil? is one of them. Is God responsible for the evil in this world; our trials, tribulations, temptations, and the like?

Jesus clarified the intentions of Satan: "The thief comes only to steal and kill and destroy; I have come that they may have life, and have it to the full" (John 10:10). By this epigrammatic statement, Jesus placed Himself and the enemy in contradistinction.

Again, the Lord Jesus defined the workings of the devil, Satan, as being without truth and filled with lies to deceive. And humans sometimes join the devil in his activity to distort and pervert truth. "You belong to your father, the devil, and you want to carry out your father's desires. He was a murderer from the beginning, not holding to the truth, for there is no truth in him. When he lies, he speaks his native language, for he is a liar and the father of lies" (John 8:44).

In other words, the devil is a lying murderer who seeks to destroy God and assume sovereignty of heaven, earth, and all that God has created. Thus, the great controversy theme is reflected in the book of Job from the first chapter.

Longtime Bible students will remember—for who could forget—the great war fought in the very holy streets of heaven. It is the beginning of what Adventists refer to as the great controversy.

The prophets Isaiah and Ezekiel and the apostle John provide detailed information about the fall of Lucifer and his transformation into Satan. There is enough for us to piece together an understanding of what happened and why.

> How you have fallen from heaven,
>   morning star, son of the dawn!
> You have been cast down to the earth,
>   you who once laid low the nations!
> You said in your heart,
>   "I will ascend to the heavens;
> I will raise my throne
>   above the stars of God;
> I will sit enthroned on the mount of assembly,
>   on the utmost heights of Mount Zaphon.
> I will ascend above the tops of the clouds;
>   I will make myself like the Most High."
> But you are brought down to the realm of the dead,
>   to the depths of the pit (Isaiah 14:12–15).

Notice that this being is referred to here as the "morning star." In the Latin vulgate, an ancient translation of Scripture often used by scholars and theologians in their biblical research, this is translated as "Lucifer," literally meaning "star of the morning."

This creature once had an exalted state as a covering cherub, close to God, until he chose to try to elevate himself above Almighty God and take His throne, trying to replace the Most High. He attempted a hostile takeover of heaven, but he was defeated and cast into the earth.

"Then war broke out in heaven. Michael and His angels fought against the dragon, and the dragon and his angels fought back. But he was not strong enough, and they lost their place in heaven. The great dragon was hurled down—that ancient serpent called the devil, or Satan, who leads the whole world astray. He was hurled to the earth, and his angels with him" (Revelation 12:7–9).

The great controversy, the war between God and Satan, began in heaven because the angel Lucifer would not submit to the authority of God. He was defeated and cast out, and now he leads the whole world astray.

What began this great war? Ezekiel 28 is a prophetic pronouncement against the King of Tyre. However, biblical expositors have also found in it a statement against the former angelic being that stood in the presence of God but was ejected therefrom.

> "You were the seal of perfection,
>   full of wisdom and perfect in beauty.
> You were in Eden,
>   the garden of God;
> every precious stone adorned you:
>   carnelian, chrysolite and emerald,
>   topaz, onyx and jasper,
>   lapis lazuli, turquoise and beryl.
> Your settings and mountings were made of gold;
>   on the day you were created they were prepared.
> You were anointed as a guardian cherub,
>   for so I ordained you.
> You were on the holy mount of God;
>   you walked among the fiery stones.

You were blameless in your ways
    from the day you were created
    till wickedness was found in you.
Through your widespread trade
    you were filled with violence,
    and you sinned.
So I drove you in disgrace from the mount of God,
    and I expelled you, guardian cherub,
    from among the fiery stones.
Your heart became proud
    on account of your beauty,
and you corrupted your wisdom
    because of your splendor.
So I threw you to the earth;
    I made a spectacle of you before kings" (Ezekiel
      28:12–17).

So here we have a brief history of Satan. He was a gloriously beautiful created being who became filled with pride over his intelligence, physical beauty, and more, none of which he had a part in creating! He was a covering cherub, as ordained by God, who had the privilege of being in the presence of God until, mysteriously wickedness or iniquity and sin were revealed within him.

In actuality, the devil created himself. He was gloriously made and filled with the capacity to love, worship, and serve God intelligently throughout eternity. Though Lucifer was originally created to bring glory and service to God—by yielding to the impulses of his own heart, he turned himself from a pristine being to one who was worthy of being cast out of heaven and into the earth.

Thus, he enters the story of Job. The first two chapters of Job describe a meeting of God with His sons (Job 1:6, 7; 2:1), "One day the angels came to present themselves before the LORD, and Satan also came with them. The Lord said to Satan, 'Where have you come from?' Satan answered the LORD, 'From roaming throughout the earth, going back and forth on it.' "

Many Bible expositors, theologians, and scholars believe that the sons of God referred to in the King James Version are actually angels as stated in the New International Version and other translations.

The location of this meeting is unknown. However, it is highly unlikely that this gathering was in heaven. Furthermore, Ellen White wrote the following, obviously describing a scene from a vision she had received and detailing part of the history of Satan:

Satan trembled as he viewed his work. He was alone in meditation upon the past, the present, and his future plans. His mighty frame shook as with a tempest. An angel from heaven was passing. He called him and entreated an interview with Christ. This was granted him. He then related to the Son of God that he repented of his rebellion and wished again the favor of God. He was willing to take the place God had previously assigned him, and be under His wise command. Christ wept at Satan's woe but told him, as the mind of God, that he could never be received into heaven. Heaven must not be placed in jeopardy. All heaven would be marred should he be received back, for sin and rebellion originated with him.[3]

Again she states a few paragraphs later:

God knew that such determined rebellion would not remain inactive. Satan would invent means to annoy the heavenly angels and show contempt for His authority. As he could not gain admission within the gates of heaven, he would wait just at the entrance, to taunt the angels and seek contention with them as they went in and out. He would seek to destroy the happiness of Adam and Eve. He would endeavor to incite them to rebellion, knowing that this would cause grief in heaven.[4]

From the above statement, we can infer that the meetings described in Job 1 and 2 did not occur in heaven. At these meetings, Satan obviously presented himself as a representative of the planet Earth, and God's response was to ask him whether he had considered Job (see Job 1:8).

Satan accepted this as a challenge and told God that Job's loyalty was purchased. God was accused, in essence, of bribery.

The conflict here presented is over rulership, worship, and loyalty. In his attempt to secure these, Satan misrepresented God to the angelic host of heaven, to Eve in the Garden of Eden, and to every human being who has lived since, including you and me.

And the only person who can successfully rebuke the devil is God! (See Zechariah 3:2.) The New Testament tells us to "resist the devil, and he will flee from you" (James 4:7, KJV).

Jesus repulsed the devil in the wilderness by correctly quoting scripture (see Matthew 4:1–11). Those words broke the power of Satan then and will do so today and forever.

Jesus is our example in the great controversy. He cast the devil, Satan, out of control by dying on the cross and paying the redemption price as the innocent bystander prophesied in Genesis 3:15—His righteous, untainted sacrifice. And by His death on the cross of Calvary, He continuously draws all people to Himself as Savior (John 12:31, 32). As He cast out Satan from heaven, He casts him out of our lives as we allow Jesus to exercise sovereignty in our lives.

Jesus enables us to overcome by being cleansed by His blood, by the recounting of our testimony to His overcoming power as our Lord and Savior. He justifies us because of our faith in who He is and what He has done and because of our confidence in what He shall yet do for us. Jesus destroys the devil's power by His mighty victory over death, hell, and the grave. The result is a victorious person who seeks to obey all of God's will.

In summary, while Job's blamelessness means mature and not perfect, his outstanding life made him an example God could use to rebuff Satan's claim to be a worthy representative of Earth. Satan could not attack Job without God's permission. God has a right to protect His property, and as Creator and Redeemer, those who yield to His authority, love, grace, and mercy fall under His protective care (see Revelation 7:1–3; Psalms 91:7; 143:9).

This episode reveals the great controversy that envelops the entire world, from Eden to the earth made new. Each of us will be tested, tempted, and tried in this life. And although we may not in this life have an answer to the four interrogatories what, why, when, or how, we can know that God—"the who," if you please—is watching over us at all times.

1. Elisha Hoffman, "Leaning on the Everlasting Arms," 1887, public domain.

2. See Psalm 139:8.

3. Ellen G. White, *The Story of Redemption* (Takoma Park, Md.: Review and Herald®, 1947), 26.

4. Ibid., 27.

CHAPTER 3

Fearing God

The first biblical notice of fear is found in Genesis 3:10, when Adam responded to God's inquiry, "Where are you?" by saying he was afraid, or fearful, of God's presence represented by His voice due to their nakedness. He was obviously filled with anxiety over what God would do.

Sin, and its attendant guilt, caused Adam to fear God. There is no earlier record of any type of fear at all prior to sin's entrance into the Garden of Eden.

Today, we have specialists who have categorized types of and given us names for specific fears and phobias: for example, acrophobia, the fear of heights; or hydrophobia, the irrational or extreme fear of water.

And fear is not all bad; if I saw a lion charging me on a city street (unlikely), the fear would cause adrenaline to course quickly through my body, and I would attempt to run before inevitably being caught. More likely, fear of injury prompts me to fasten the seat belt when I get into my car.

But in the context of fearing God, the Bible usually means something altogether different from a common fear of an enemy or an extreme and irrational fear, such as a phobia. The Bible frequently uses the words *God-fearing* and *fear God*. But what does the Bible mean when it uses this or similar terminology?

After all, Job is described at the beginning of the book as being God-fearing.

Often times in the Old Testament, God fearers are not just ones who are *afraid* of God but ones who hold God in awe and reverence. How else would one be able to serve God rightly without being coerced by fear of destruction? The element of fear disqualifies the service from being legitimate, because it is self-centered and not God-centered.

To be sure, the Bible from Genesis through Revelation paints a picture of a God who is the Almighty One who hates and consumes sin and seeks to destroy it one day. But to be God-fearing in the sense that it is spoken of in the book of Job is to have a complete loyalty to God, born of the deep awe and profound respect due to Him. This respect is not born of a fear of destruction but one that comes from a desire to please one's Creator—it is the product of a relationship.

Fearing God is part of the three angels' messages, as the first angel calls us to fear God and give glory to Him because He is the Creator. "He said in a loud voice, 'Fear God and give Him glory, because the hour of His judgment has come. Worship Him who made the heavens, the earth, the sea and the springs of water' " (Revelation 12:7).

A God-fearing person is a pious person, devoted and dedicated to God and His plan for our lives. And this particular God-fearing man became the target of Satan's anger at God. It was because of Job's love and loyal obedience to God that Satan rightly stated that God had placed a hedge—a hedge of protection—around Job.

This term, *hedge,* could be likened to a fence or wall around a compound or a house. God blessed Job because of his integrity, which is a conscious choice; God is a being of integrity, and He wants His people to be like Him.

Let me illustrate. Many of us have alarm systems on our cars and/or in our homes, and when we leave our homes or vehicles, we activate those devices. If we do not have the electronic devices, we use the old fashioned locks. We are simply seeking to protect our property while we are away. The Bible is full of statements about thieves, and they are found in every neighborhood. Someday, in the earth made new, those devices or locks will be unnecessary because there will no longer be thieves; but in this life, we feel more comfortable using them to protect our belongings.

And there is nothing wrong with protecting our property, which we have invested in. It would be foolish not to do so.

Likewise, God seeks to protect His "property"—His children, in whom He has invested the blood of His own dear Son. While we are not things, our heavenly Father values our lives and seeks to protect us within the grand scheme of the great controversy. That does not mean that nothing bad will ever befall us; it just means that God controls the activity of the evil one in our lives.

The hedge in the narrative also indicates that the enemy has limited access to our lives. It was only after Satan's nefarious accusation against God through the subtext of criticizing Job that God said, "Behold, all that he has is in your power; only do not lay a hand on his person" (Job 1:12, NKJV).

Remember, Satan essentially stated that God had bribed Job, which not only reduces Job to a "hireling" but also implies that God is willing to buy the love, loyalty, and worship of humanity— a claim that cannot be substantiated, yet one to which God responded.

Why does anyone serve God? If it is because of the blessings we hope to receive from the hand of our Creator, is that a legitimate reason to do so? Romans 2:4b indicates "God's kindness is intended to lead [us] to repentance."

As we review the operation of grace in our lives today, we realize that God has been good to us (an understatement to be sure) and that, as Paul tells us, leads us to repentance. And true, godly repentance leads us to the foot of the cross of Christ to confess our sins and turn from our fallen, evil ways and to pledge loyalty to Jesus Christ.

When I was a child attending grammar school, we started the day by reciting the Pledge of Allegiance. We did so with our hats removed, standing tall and straight with our right hands over our hearts. In it, we pledged loyalty to our country. "I pledge allegiance to the flag of the United States of America, and to the republic for which it stands, one nation under God, indivisible, with liberty and justice for all."

There is also a version of a pledge of allegiance to the Christian flag:[1] I pledge allegiance to the Christian flag and to the Savior for whose kingdom it stands. One Savior, crucified, risen, and coming again with life and liberty to all who believe.

Our lives are to be a pledge of allegiance to God and His mercy, grace, and protection, all of which are byproducts of His great love for us. As we "grow in the grace and knowledge of our Lord and Savior Jesus Christ" (2 Peter 3:18), we are able to perceive more clearly what God is about in our lives and in the world around us, not because we are smart enough to figure it out but because God reveals Himself to us in an ever-expanding manner.

As we become more and more sensitive to the Holy Spirit's activity, we understand more of what God reveals to us about Himself and learn there is much more to serving God than doing so only to receive His blessings.

With all of his temporal blessings removed, Job still maintained his commitment, his pledge of allegiance, if you will, to God.

I cannot imagine the grief parents experience when a child precedes them in death. It is unnatural, even in this world. Job's first set of children do not die naturally but are killed, not one by one, but all at once.

How does Job respond? In a simple statement of fact that appears incomprehensible to us:

> "Naked I came from my mother's womb,
>   and naked I will depart.
> The LORD gave and the LORD has taken away;
>   may the name of the LORD be praised."
> In all this, Job did not sin by charging God with wrong-
>   doing (Job 1:20–22).

As one commentator puts it: "Recognizing God's sovereign rights (*The Lord gave and the Lord has taken away*), Job *praised* the

Lord. It is truly remarkable that Job followed adversity with adoration, woe with worship. Unlike so many people, he did not give in to bitterness; he refused to blame *God* for *wrongdoing* (cf. Job 2:10)."[2]

This is a testimony to the faith of a God-fearing man. Job does not bemoan the evil that came upon him, nor does he blame or curse God. He simply stated a universal fact for all humanity. We are born with no possessions, and all the possessions we accumulate through our lives will be left behind when we die.

As a free moral agent, a person capable of making his own decisions, Job proved so loyal to God that he won round one in his struggle with the enemy.

But, the devil wasn't finished; he actually approached the assembly of the angels again, as recorded in Job 2:1–3.

His opening "gambit" failed, so he ups the ante, as it were. He doubles down, in gambling terms, in the face of God and the sons of God, or angelic witnesses.

It is not enough that Satan attacks Job without provocation, taking his material goods and his children.

He now asks for permission to touch Job's body, to inflict him with disease. Satan, true to form, seeks to destroy any and all who are loyal to God. Knowing that he cannot hurt God directly, having lost the war fought in heaven, he seeks to hurt God indirectly, by causing pain and destruction to come upon God's children.

And in the second round, God once again challenges Satan with the best representative of earth, Job. Once again, in the presence of the "sons of God," Satan "calls God out"—Satan challenges God by asking for permission to touch Job's body, to inflict pain upon him in an attempt to get him to release his faith in God. God allows it, and the enemy brings intense physical pain on Job:

> "Skin for skin!" Satan replied. "A man will give all he has for his own life. But now stretch out your hand and strike his flesh and bones, and he will surely curse you to your face."

> The Lord said to Satan, "Very well, then, he is in your hands; but you must spare his life."
>
> So Satan went out from the presence of the Lord and afflicted Job with painful sores from the soles of his feet to the crown of his head (Job 2:4–7).

While we don't have a diagnosis of Job's sickness, we do know it was demonically initiated and was so intense that he sat on a heap of ashes and scraped the puss from the oozing sores, which covered him from head to toe. What a scene.

And yet, Job remained faithful to God! Remember Paul's assessment of faith in Hebrews 11:6? "But without faith it is impossible to please Him, for he who comes to God must believe that He is, and that He is a rewarder of those who diligently seek him" (NKJV).

When we think of Job's response to his trials in comparison to Adam and Eve in their temptation, we would note that Adam and Eve were tempted in a perfect world, one without sin and depravity. They failed their test.

Job's world, like ours today, was steeped in sin and evil, and he "passed" the test.

Presumably, Adam and Eve had seen the universal Creator face to face; Job hadn't. And, both Adam and Eve sought to "pass the buck": Adam blamed Eve, Eve blamed the serpent, and in doing so they both implicated God, making Him responsible for their choice to disobey and plunge the world into sinful disobedience.

Job worshiped and mourned, without blaming God.

While Job is the hero of the tale, Mrs. Job was there too. She is the one who gave birth to the ten children who were destroyed. She was the first teacher of her children, like all women in biblical times. And, she lost everything that she enjoyed in the death of her children. Here, Job's faith shone forth as a beacon in the deepest darkness of suffering. In this, Job symbolically portrays the sufferings of Christ. Both were attacked without provocation—the attacks undeserved and unwarranted. Jesus was also attacked by the prince of darkness. He suffered, bled, and died at

Calvary as an innocent bystander, the true Lamb of God offered up for the sins of the world (see John 3:16, 17). And like Job, Jesus did not accuse God; He remained faithful to the end.

As Louisa Stead, her husband, and their little daughter were enjoying an oceanside picnic one day, a drowning boy cried for help. Mr. Stead rushed to save him but was pulled under by the terrified boy. Both drowned as Louisa and her daughter watched helplessly.

Soon after this Mrs. Stead and her daughter left for missionary work in South Africa. After more than twenty-five years of fruitful service, Louisa was forced to retire because of ill health. She died a few years later in Southern Rhodesia (now named Zimbabwe). Her fellow missionaries had always loved " 'Tis So Sweet to Trust in Jesus" and wrote this tribute after her death:

Out of a deep human tragedy early in her life, Louisa Stead learned simply to trust in her Lord. She was used up to "the praise of His glory" for the remainder of her life. Still today, her ministry continues each time we sing and apply the truth of these words:

'Tis so sweet to trust in Jesus, just to take Him at His word, just to rest upon His promise, just to know, "Thus saith the Lord."

O how sweet to trust in Jesus, just to trust His cleansing blood, just in simple faith to plunge me 'neath the healing, cleansing flood!

Yes, 'tis sweet to trust in Jesus, just from sin and self to cease, just from Jesus simply taking life and rest and joy and peace.

I'm so glad I learned to trust Thee, Precious Jesus, Savior, Friend; and I know that Thou art with me, wilt be with me to the end.

Chorus: Jesus, Jesus, how I trust Him! How I've proved Him o'er and o'er! Jesus, Jesus, precious Jesus! O for grace to trust Him more![3]

Even though Job suffered intensely, he learned to trust God

completely and maintained his integrity. He was able to say, "Though he slay me, yet will I trust in him: but I will maintain my own ways before Him" (Job 13:15, KJV).

1. "Pledge to the Christian Flag," ChristianHomeschoolers.com, http://www .christianhomeschoolers.com/christian_pledges.html.

2. Roy B. Zuck, "Job," in *The Bible Knowledge Commentary: An Exposition of the Scriptures,* ed. John F. Walvoord and Roy B. Zuck, vol. 1 (Wheaton, Ill.: Victor Books, 1985), 720, 721; emphasis added.

3. K. W. Osbeck, *Amazing Grace: 366 Inspiring Hymn Stories for Daily Devotions* (Grand Rapids, Mich.: Kregel Publications, 1996), 220.

CHAPTER 4

God and Human Suffering

The great controversy explains the universal presence of evil. As a result, the totality of humanity suffers; the characteristics may vary, but suffering comes to everyone. The book of Job is the oldest book in the Bible. In its pages, God addresses the great controversy and how to successfully deal with the issue of our pain and suffering.

It is important that we remember that God Himself suffers. He suffers while watching sin ravage His creation. He suffered when Jesus entered this world and when He went to the cross of Calvary. But there was no "plan B" for the salvation of the world, and Jesus voluntarily embraced His calling to shed His innocent blood and die for the salvation of mankind.

As we work through the book of Job, there is seemingly a multitude of questions that beg to be answered. Who taught Job how to worship God? For that matter, how did Job come to the conclusion that God even existed? Where did Job learn to provide the sacrificial offerings that were a shadow of the coming Christ? The Bible doesn't tell us.

However, the Bible does teach us that the natural world points us to God as our Creator. "For since the creation of the world God's invisible qualities—his eternal power and divine nature—have been clearly seen, being understood from what has been made, so that people are without excuse" (Romans 1:20). Truth is proclaimed in the visible world. In other words, Paul is saying that God will take vengeance on sin in view of the fact that people have had the opportunity in all ages to observe God's character through the world He has created.

Consider this: "Nature and revelation alike testify of God's love. Our Father in heaven is the source of life, of wisdom, and of joy. Look at the wonderful and beautiful things of nature. Think of their marvelous adaptation to the needs and happiness, not only of man, but of all living creatures. The sunshine and the rain, that gladden and refresh the earth, the hills and seas and plains, all speak to us of the Creator's love. It is God who supplies the daily needs of all His creatures."[1]

When we compare Job 12:7–10 with Romans 1:16–20, we find Paul agreeing with Job over the distance of thousands of years. The two authors agree that nature reveals its origins; God is given the credit for the creation.

And of course, nothing creates itself. The very design of everything in nature reveals the element of intelligent design and not mutation or survival of the fittest as evolutionists maintain.

In natural theology, a cosmological argument is an argument in which the existence of a unique being, generally identified with or referred to as God, is deduced or inferred as highly probable from facts or alleged facts concerning causation, change, motion, contingency, or finitude in respect of the universe as a whole or processes within it. It is traditionally known as an argument from universal causation, an argument from first cause, the causal argument or the argument from existence. Whichever term is employed, there are three basic variants of the argument, each with subtle yet important distinctions: the arguments from *in causa* (causality), *in esse* (essentially), and *in fieri* (becoming).

The basic premise of all of these is the concept of causality and of a First Cause. The history of this argument goes back to Aristotle or earlier, was developed in

Neoplatonism and early Christianity and later in medieval Islamic theology during the 9th to 12th centuries, and re-introduced to medieval Christian theology in the 13th century. The cosmological argument is closely related to the principle of sufficient reason as discussed by Gottfried Leibniz and Samuel Clarke, itself a modern exposition of the claim that "Nothing comes from nothing" attributed to Parmenides.

Contemporary defenders or partial defenders of cosmological arguments include William Lane Craig, Robert Koons, Alexander Pruss, and William L. Rowe.[2]

However, Revelation 4:11 clearly states:

> "You are worthy, our Lord and God,
>   to receive glory and honor and power,
> for you created all things,
>   and by your will they were created
>   and have their being."

God is worthy of our highest praise, adoration and worship, glory and honor—for many reasons—but prominently and precisely because He is the Creator of all things, and everything that exists was created for the purpose God created them for: to bring Him pleasure.

In Colossians 1:16, 17 Paul is more explicit, giving a list of the effects of the Creator's activity: "For in him all things were created: things in heaven and on earth, visible and invisible, whether thrones or powers or rulers or authorities; all things have been created through him and for him. He is before all things, and in him all things hold together."

In this verse Paul provided the reason for asserting the supremacy of Christ over creation. The three phrases "in him" (v. 16a), "through him" (v. 16b), and "for him" (v. 16b) indicate the relationship. In actuality, three different ideas are expressed by these phrases. The first of these is the Greek expression translated literally "in him." It should be understood as in His mind or in His sphere of influence and responsibility. Practically, it means that Jesus conceived of creation and its complexities—creation was His idea.[3]

Here Paul tells us all things in totality were created by Jesus Christ, not only things in the heavens (stars, planets etc.), easily visible things, but also those that are unseen by our unaided eye (microbes, atoms, and the like); thrones that rulers sit on, and the territories that comprise their kingdoms. Everything. Period.

John 1:1–3 states, "In the beginning was the Word, and the Word was with God, and the Word was God. He was with God in the beginning. Through him all things were made; without him nothing was made that has been made."

Very simplistically stated, the apostle John wrote that the Word, understood as Jesus, is fully God and was with God the Father before the creation of this world took place. Nothing in the world was created or came into existence from nothing except as Jesus created it.

Any so-called wisdom that is disconnected from the Source of all knowledge is counted as foolishness. First Corinthians 3:18–20 states it clearly: "Do not deceive yourselves. If any of you think you are wise by the standards of this age, you should become 'fools' so that you may become wise. For the wisdom of this world is foolishness in God's sight. As it is written: 'He catches the wise in their craftiness'; and again, 'The Lord knows that the thoughts of the wise are futile.' "

Here Paul even quotes from Job 5:13, accepting the book of Job as being valid for teaching about God and His operations. While Paul's statement is contextualized—that is, relevant to his time and the philosophy of his culture—the Bible clearly opposes all teaching that is "anti"-God.

The superiority of God's true wisdom is stated throughout the Bible. Consider Isaiah 55:8, 9:

> "For my thoughts are not your thoughts,
>   neither are your ways my ways,"
>   declares the Lord.
> "As the heavens are higher than the earth,

so are my ways higher than your ways
and my thoughts than your thoughts."

If we believe that the Creator knows more than we do, we must accept the teachings given by the inspiration of the Holy Spirit.

Many commentators and biblical expositors express the belief that Moses wrote the book of Job during the forty years of his sojourn in Midian after fleeing Egypt as a princely murderer. "Others argue that it was written by Job himself, or by Elihu, or Isaiah, or perhaps more probably by Moses, who was 'learned in all the wisdom of the Egyptians, and mighty in words and deeds' (Acts 7:22). He had opportunities in Midian for obtaining the knowledge of the facts related."[4]

The pen of inspiration writes, "Not only was Moses gaining a preparation for the great work before him, but during this time, under the inspiration of the Holy Spirit, he wrote the book of Genesis and also the book of Job, which would be read with the deepest interest by the people of God until the close of time."[5]

While we can only know what God reveals of His plans for us, it may be safe to assume that God, looking at the needs of His people, inspired Moses to write the book of Job because God knew we would need it during the entire time of our existence in a world grasped by evil. Through Job, God informs us that He is with us and that we are not left alone to endure pain and suffering.

The reality of evil is addressed in the Bible from cover to cover. After Jesus speaks about helping the needy, prayer and fasting, and where our true treasures should be placed, Matthew records Jesus as summarizing what our approach to life's practical concerns should be in the following: "Therefore do not worry about tomorrow, for tomorrow will worry about itself. Each day has enough trouble of its own" (Matthew 6:34).

Back in the early 1970s, I saw a statement on a poster board that went something like this: "Worry is like being in a rocking chair; it uses a lot of energy but doesn't get you anywhere."[6] I think this statement is true, and it reflects what Jesus taught in

Matthew 6:27: "Can any one of you by worrying add a single hour to your life?" This may have been the classic rhetorical question.

We do not lengthen our lives or add quality to our existence by worrying. This doesn't mean that we do not have concerns or make plans by preparing for what may be eventualities, but we are not to be consumed by trying to figure out what is going to happen or by pining over what has happened. The key is to obey God in the present and trust the future and the past to His hand.

While we are instructed not to worry about the evil coming in the future (Matthew 6:34), we are reminded that Jesus has already overcome the tribulation in the world and offers us peace in the midst of the storm of evil that surrounds and follows us (John 16:33).

Both Paul and Peter, among other biblical writers, reflect this teaching of our Lord. In Philippians 4:6–7, Paul writes, "Do not be anxious about anything, but in every situation, by prayer and petition, with thanksgiving, present your requests to God. And the peace of God, which transcends all understanding, will guard your hearts and your minds in Christ Jesus." And in 1 Peter 5:7, Peter writes, "Cast all your anxiety on him because he cares for you."

Certainly Jesus' advice in Matthew 6:34 does not negate a loving God; it acknowledges, however, the reality of this fallen world and hints at the real problem of reconciling a loving, all-powerful God with his seeming tolerance or inability to remove the evil of pain and suffering from His world. This is the question of theodicy, the vindication of divine goodness and providence in view of the existence of evil.

Job is the fullest development in Scripture of the issue referred to by theologians and philosophers as "the problem of evil" or "theodicy." The question is, What kind of God allows the seemingly innocent to experience evil, pain, and suffering? Logic suggests one of three answers: (1) God is righteous, but He is not powerful enough to prevent suffering; (2) God is all-powerful, but He is not truly good and has elements of evil in His nature; or (3) all pain and evil is in fact deserved by the sufferer and sent by God (in other words, the truly innocent do not suffer).

The biblical view finds these answers unacceptable, and the book of Job wrestles with the alternative by providing a wider perspective. The conflict of the ages between God and Satan must demonstrate the righteousness and supremacy of God. He lets the innocent suffer to demonstrate that in His sovereignty, He receives glory even when His people suffer and persevere in faith without understanding why. From a merely human point of view, the answer is that no answer is given to the problem of evil. From a divine perspective, the answer is that God's glory is served even when evil is permitted. (Christ's death is God's ultimate answer to the problem of evil.) Those who study Job today should interpret it in view of its original purpose.[7]

Job praised God in the midst of his trials and tribulation (see Job 1:20, 21; 2:10)—even though he struggled with questions, such as, Why is God allowing this? Why is God sending this? These were among the questions that plagued him; though his faith in God wavered, it didn't fail. Instead, Job bravely stated, "Though He slay me, yet will I trust in him: but I will maintain mine own ways before him" (Job 13:15, KJV).

In his thinking, and frequently in ours, he was innocent of any transgression that would justifiably warrant his suffering. While Job never doubts God's existence, he doubted, temporarily, His character. Many of us do so today. However, we have what Job could only see dimly. We have a clear demonstration of God's character reflected in the suffering of Jesus on the cross.

> Few give thought to the suffering that sin has caused our Creator. All heaven suffered in Christ's agony; but that suffering did not begin or end with His manifestation in humanity. The cross is a revelation to our dull senses of the pain that, from its very inception, sin has brought to the heart of God. Every departure from the right, every deed of cruelty, every failure of humanity to reach His ideal, brings grief to Him. When there came upon Israel the calamities that were the sure result of separation from God—subjugation by their enemies, cruelty, and

death,—it is said that "His soul was grieved for the misery of Israel." "In all their affliction He was afflicted: . . . and He bare them, and carried them all the days of old." (Judges 10:16; Isaiah 63:9).[8]

The cross of Christ shows us that God is willing to suffer with us to redeem us; therefore, He can be trusted.

---

1. Ellen G. White, *Steps to Christ* (Nampa, Idaho: Pacific Press®, 1999), 9.

2. "Cosmological Argument," *Wikipedia,* last updated September 12, 2015, https://en.wikipedia.org/wiki/cosmological_argument.

3. Richard R. Melick, *Philippians, Colossians, Philemon,* vol. 32, The New American Commentary (Nashville, Tenn.: Broadman & Holman, 1991), 217.

4. M. G. Easton, "Job, Book of," *Easton's Bible Dictionary* (New York: Harper & Brothers, 1893).

5. Ellen G. White, "Moses," *Signs of the Times,* February 19, 1880, 73.

6. A Google search quotes a version of this statement in a statement in a movie by Van Wilder in 2002, but I saw the statement thirty years earlier.

7. K. H. Easley, *Holman QuickSource Guide to Understanding the Bible* (Nashville, Tenn.: Holman Bible Publishers, 2002), 112.

8. Ellen G. White, *Education* (Mountain View, Calif.: Pacific Press®, 1952), 263.

CHAPTER 5

Curse the Day

"After this, Job opened his mouth and cursed the day of his birth" (Job 3:1). Just prior to this, Job was gripped with the most horrible experience imaginable: all of his earthly goods were stolen or destroyed; his ten children and any hopes of a progeny to continue his name and lineage in the earth died a horrible death; and finally, he was touched with foul, loathsome, sore boils from which he can see no cure. And in her grief, his wife tells him to "curse God and die." Wow.

He lost his wealth, children, and health, but, worse yet, at this time he has no understanding of why he is suffering. The Bible record states that Job cursed the day of his birth; this blameless, upright, and God-fearing man curses.

Hold on a moment . . . there is no indication that what Job states bears any resemblance to the bad language or expletives that we hear cast into the air when people are angry or excited today. No "four-letter" words that are part of the common vernacular of the day, which are unsuitable, in my opinion, for Christians to say.

Job's expression and his detailed speech come from the depths of the despair that he was experiencing. In his place, we would likely do the same—or worse. Job's pain was so deep and intense that he desired his birthday to be ripped from the historical calendar.

It is important to note what Job did not do at this juncture: he does not blame or curse God, although some might argue that to curse the day of his birth was indirectly cursing God. As Creator, He made the day and not only planned and executed the moment of his conception but also caused him to enter the world right on time.

Maybe Solomon was familiar with the book of Job when he wrote these words:

> And I declared that the dead,
>   who had already died,
> are happier than the living,
>   who are still alive.
> But better than both
>   is the one who has never been born,
> who has not seen the evil
>   that is done under the sun (Ecclesiastes 4:2, 3).

Or the prophet Jeremiah, who wrote, referencing his own suffering:

> Cursed be the day I was born!
>   May the day my mother bore me not be blessed!
> Cursed be the man who brought my father the news,
>   who made him very glad, saying,
>   "A child is born to you—a son!"
> May that man be like the towns
>   the Lord overthrew without pity.
> May he hear wailing in the morning,
>   a battle cry at noon.
> For he did not kill me in the womb,
>   with my mother as my grave,
>   her womb enlarged forever.
> Why did I ever come out of the womb
>   to see trouble and sorrow
>   and to end my days in shame? (Jeremiah 20:14–18).

One commentary states, relative to Job's cursing: "His execrations are solemn, deep, and sublime. These poetic statements do not lend themselves to minute technical analysis. Job is not presenting logic. Rather, he is pouring out the impassioned feelings of a suffering soul."[1]

Remember, Job had a distinct disadvantage: he didn't know *why*. This leads us to think that his physical suffering, while deep, was eclipsed by his mental anguish.

We, living thousands of years after Job and with the advantage of the historical account of his life, know how the entire sorry tale started. We also know, at a glance, how it ends. In addition, we have the New Testament teaching on suffering to help us in the struggle to understand suffering in general and our own suffering in particular, through the lens of faith and trust in God.

We recognize the motif of the Suffering Servant and His role in our redemption, found in Isaiah 53:

> Who has believed our message
> and to whom has the arm of the LORD been revealed?
> He grew up before him like a tender shoot,
> and like a root out of dry ground.
> He had no beauty or majesty to attract us to him,
> nothing in his appearance that we should desire him.
> He was despised and rejected by mankind,
> a man of suffering, and familiar with pain.
> Like one from whom people hide their faces
> he was despised, and we held him in low esteem.
> Surely he took up our pain
> and bore our suffering,
> yet we considered him punished by God,
> stricken by him, and afflicted.
> But he was pierced for our transgressions,
> he was crushed for our iniquities;
> the punishment that brought us peace was on him,
> and by his wounds we are healed.
> We all, like sheep, have gone astray,
> each of us has turned to our own way;

and the LORD has laid on him
    the iniquity of us all.
He was oppressed and afflicted,
    yet he did not open his mouth;
he was led like a lamb to the slaughter,
    and as a sheep before its shearers is silent,
    so he did not open his mouth.
By oppression and judgment he was taken away.
    Yet who of his generation protested?
For he was cut off from the land of the living;
    for the transgression of my people he was punished.
He was assigned a grave with the wicked,
    and with the rich in His death,
though he had done no violence,
    nor was any deceit in his mouth.
Yet it was the LORD's will to crush him and cause him to
    suffer,
    and though the LORD makes his life an offering for sin,
he will see His offspring and prolong his days,
    and the will of the LORD will prosper in his hand.
After he has suffered,
    he will see the light of life and be satisfied;
by his knowledge my righteous servant will justify many,
    and he will bear their iniquities.
Therefore I will give him a portion among the great,
    and he will divide the spoils with the strong,
because he poured out his life unto death,
    and was numbered with the transgressors.
For he bore the sin of many,
    and made intercession for the transgressors (Isaiah
        53:1–12).

Consider this statement:

As soon as there was sin, there was a Saviour. Christ
knew that He would have to suffer, yet He became man's
substitute. As soon as Adam sinned, the Son of God pre-

sented Himself as surety for the human race.

Think of how much it cost Christ to leave the heavenly courts, and take His position at the head of humanity. Why did He do this? Because He was the only one who could redeem the fallen race. There was not a human being in the world who was without sin. The Son of God stepped down from His heavenly throne, laid off His royal robe and kingly crown, and clothed His divinity with humanity. He came to die for us, to lie in the tomb as human beings must, and to be raised for our justification. He came to become acquainted with all the temptations wherewith man is beset. He rose from the grave and proclaimed over the rent sepulcher of Joseph, "I am the resurrection, and the life." One equal with God passed through death in our behalf. He tasted death for every man, that through Him every man might be a partaker of eternal life.[2]

While we will not at this time develop a full exposition of Isaiah 53, Christians—generally speaking—recognize this to be a prophetic revelation of the role of Jesus Christ in partial fulfillment of Genesis 3:15.

But what did Job hope death would do for him? Since this is the oldest book in the Bible, surely the One who inspired its writing had something to reveal regarding the state of the dead. Job 3:13 states, "For now I would be lying down in peace; I would be asleep and at rest."

Clearly, Job expected to be at rest from his trials, troubles, and tribulations. He stated plainly that he would be asleep and at rest. No mention of an expected visit to heaven and an immediate reward for his blameless, upright, God-fearing life. Not one word.

Of course, we do not build a theological understanding on one part of Scripture but, instead, compare scripture with scripture (see Isaiah 28:10), and thus a pattern of truth is uncovered or revealed. Job's statement is consistent with the multitude of biblical information on the state of the dead. Let's look at a few other passages from the sacred Scripture:

For the living know that they will die;
But the dead know nothing,
And they have no more reward,
For the memory of them is forgotten.
Also their love, their hatred, and their envy have now
    perished;
Nevermore will they have a share
In anything done under the sun (Ecclesiastes 9:5, 6,
    NKJV).

Solomon, "the wisest man to ever live," simply states that while we are alive, we are aware, and we can think, plan, and act. We have the knowledge of what we will do, but, in contrast, the dead don't know a thing. All their emotions are passed away, and they have nothing else to do in the affairs of life.

Do you show your wonders to the dead?
    Do their spirits rise up and praise you?
Is your love declared in the grave,
    your faithfulness in Destruction?
Are your wonders known in the place of darkness,
    or your righteous deeds in the land of oblivion? (Psalm
    88:10–12).

These rhetorical questions from Psalm 88 are intended to be answered in the negative. But what about the New Testament? What does Jesus say about death?

Perhaps one of the clearest teachings on death in the New Testament is found in John 11, where we find the story of Jesus' good friend Lazarus's death and resurrection. "By the miracle of raising Lazarus to life Jesus aimed to give crowning evidence to the disbelieving Jews that He was the Messiah, the Saviour of the world."[3]

Lazarus was dead for four days before Jesus brought him back to life. If a person gets their reward for life immediately upon death (as states the commonly held belief), surely, Lazarus would have described his "after death" experience, and that narrative would be preserved in the Bible.

There is plenty of talk today in our society that people who die have gone on to a "better place." This is not supported scripturally. The idea that a "soul" continues to exist beyond the grave is absent from a clear exposition on the Bible (see also Ezekiel 18:4 and John 5:25–29).

In death, Job anticipated a rest and escape from his current torturous existence. We may ask, if Job really wanted to die, why not commit suicide? The narrative doesn't address this subject, and an attempt to address this is futile.

Pain and suffering are unique because they are completely subjective: we can truly experience only our individual pain. We may sympathize with others and have compassion on them during their pain and suffering, but in actuality, we cannot know what their pain is like.

When we hurt, it is uniquely isolated and limited to what we are going through. As a pastor, I have visited countless homes where death has taken away a family member. As much as I may have loved the deceased, I can never fully know the depth of pain experienced by the family. I can try to put myself in their place, but in reality, I cannot.

Neither could Job's three friends who came to comfort him— Eliphaz the Temanite, Bildad the Shuhite, and Zophar the Naamathite—appreciate his pain.

When we look at Job's friends who came to comfort him and sympathize with him (Job 2:11), we see that they began with silence. Sometimes silent companionship is more important than words when visiting the suffering. Those who have been the recipient of a visit while hospitalized may appreciate more the silent support, rather than the chatter of visitors.

But the three friends departed from their seven-day "silence fast" and quickly left their position of support. In fact, they defined his pain by their belief that he was getting his reward for hidden sin.

Job comes to the place where he questions his suffering as punishment and seeks forgiveness for an "unknown" sin (Job 7:17–21). Job delivers the theological thought of his time that, as expressed much later, "the curse causeless shall not come" (Proverbs 26:2, KJV). He even delves into what one may call existentialism when he ponders what exactly are human beings and why does God interact with them. Within the great controversy, which is all about the justification of God and the restoration of order in the universe, we have the presentation of God's love for mankind. John 3:16 states it so sublimely that commenting on it is really unnecessary: "For God so loved the world, that he gave his only begotten Son, that whosoever believeth in him should not perish, but have everlasting life" (KJV).

God is love; 1 John 4:8 makes that plain. We must accept it by faith, even though we cannot see the unfolding of that fact in our world of pain and suffering. If we just look at an event, or series of events, it may be like missing the forest while looking at the tree(s).

---

1. Nichol, *The Seventh-day Adventist Bible Commentary*, vol. 3, 505.

2. Ellen G. White, *In Heavenly Places* (Takoma Park, Md.: Review and Herald®, 1967), 13.

3. Nichol, *The Seventh-day Adventist Bible Commentary*, vol. 5, 1012.

CHAPTER 6

The Curse Causeless

The title of this lesson is taken from Proverbs 26:2, "As the bird by wandering, as the swallow by flying, so the curse causeless shall not come" (KJV). Simply stated, the second part of this statement has a large measure of truth to it. Many times, we directly or indirectly bring our troubles upon ourselves. Our lifestyles, our habits, our choices, and even our hastily spoken words can often result in an event or series of events that are painful or even disastrous. And, in the context of the book of Job, that seems to be the perspective of Job's three friends.

The narrative of this profound book really opens up an opportunity to have a broadened understanding of some of the interaction between God and the devil, and how it involves us.

Job is front-loaded with action; that is to say, all the heavy stuff takes place in the first two chapters of the book. The remainder is largely made up of conversation taking place between four people: Job, Eliphaz, Bildad, and Zophar.

Job's three friends probably were wealthy like Job. If they were working-class men, they would probably not have a chance to take seven days of their prime working time to come and sit silently with their suffering friend. The book does not indicate how his three friends heard of Job's sufferings; perhaps a nomadic trading caravan that had done business with all of them had shared the news. And we do not have much information about where these cities that the three came from were located, with the exception of one: "Eliphaz came from Teman. Genesis 36:4 records a son born to Esau and Adah named Eliphaz. In turn, Teman was born to Eliphaz (Genesis 36:11). Teman came to be the name of a prominent city in the area of Edom southeast of the Dead Sea. If the identification of this and Job's location is correct, it meant for Eliphaz a journey of over a hundred miles."[1]

In order for Eliphaz to reach Job, he most likely traveled by riding a beast of burden or in a carriage drawn by animals accustomed to traveling long distances. The Bible does not state what time of year this occurred, but if it was during the unusually hot desert summer, a lengthy trip would require special planning. To the credit of Job's three friends—they came with good intentions and to support their friend or fellow businessman.

Here is a note for us: When our friends are sick, would we travel miles, though inconvenient, to comfort them? How far do we go with our own church members to let them know that we mourn with them, to the furthest extent possible?

How far did Jesus go to comfort and support us—His "friends," as he called his disciples in John 15:15b: "But I have called you friends; for all things that I have heard of my Father I have made known unto you" (KJV).

Was it convenient for the three friends of Job to travel for their suffering friend? Most likely not. We sometimes will not do things for our friends if it involves inconvenience. Or we may exit our comfort zone only for really, really close friends. These men must have been really close to Job to travel a great distance and join him in the dust and keep silent with him for seven days.

The lesson takes us to Psalm 119:65–72. Here the psalmist recognizes that God has dealt well with (His) servant while teaching him good judgment, knowledge, and discernment (see Philippians 1:9). The servant acknowledges that before his affliction, he strayed, but now after the affliction he keeps (God's) word.

After his unnamed affliction, this servant expresses what many would say is a profound appreciation for God's law, commands, and precepts.

Sometimes the best lessons are learned the hard way. Even though God seeks to guard us from the pain and punishment that comes when we break His law, it often teaches us to stay close to God.

I once heard a story of a shepherd who had a lamb that he frequently had to rescue, spending much time away from his flock to look for and retrieve the erring sheep. As the story goes, the shepherd eventually broke one of the lamb's legs. He then set it, dressed it, bandaged it, and then carried that lamb until the leg healed.

As the story goes, because that shepherd carried the lamb close to his chest, the lamb learned to love the shepherd, and when he was healed and was able to walk and run on its own, he kept especially close to the shepherd and never strayed again.

I am not sure if there is any veracity to the story—it sounds cruel and harsh. And I don't believe the Good Shepherd, Jesus (see John 10:11, 14 and Jeremiah 3:15), ever directly inflicts pain on those who follow Him. However, when we are outside of His will, often the Lord allows problems to come to us that overcome us.

Many years ago, a drunk walked into the church during our weekly prayer meeting. I watched him closely while the small group was giving testimonies, as we prayed and sang songs to God's glory.

I gave him a ride home that night, and, over some time, we developed a friendship. One day he told me his story of trials, troubles, and tribulations. He had lived through the Vietnam war, and he told me that whenever the enemy launched mortars and the United States troops could tell they were "incoming" by the unique sound they made, all of them sought the nearest fox-holes or craters created by the last fusillade of mortar shells. He said that there were no atheists in the foxholes; all of them were praying for deliverance.

However, once the rain of mortars stopped, they all returned to their former activities: off-duty boozing, drugging, and ignoring God; then he said, "danger gone, God forgotten."

At the risk of sounding judgmental, I want to underscore a

truth: fear or pain is not a permanent motivator to seek God. Only in recognizing the love that God gives can we respond to Him on a consistent basis.

Job's friends mourned with him in the custom of their time. They came to join him in his sorrow and suffering by sharing time and space with him; mourning his loss of fortune, family, and now health; and giving him their collective comfort. There are times when the tragedies of life take our breath away and the community convenes to share the grief and sorrow of the loss.

These friends sat silent, as has been pointed out earlier. But once Job spoke and cried out ruing the day of his birth, it seems that the pent-up emotion of their three days was ready to burst forth like water through an overwhelmed dam.

Perhaps Eliphaz was the natural leader of the group, like Jesus' disciple Peter, and was the first to speak. He acknowledges, perhaps indirectly, that Job had helped others who were visited by misfortune, but now that it came to his house, as it were, Job wanted to die! In the middle of his speech, Eliphaz asks, "Remember now, whoever perished being innocent? Or where were the upright destroyed?" (Job 4:7, NASB). He even infers that Job would be cut off!

Eliphaz was indeed expressing the thought of his day that you surely will receive as you have sown. Certainly this biblical principle is found in Luke 6:38, "Give, and it will be given to you. A good measure, pressed down, shaken together and running over, will be poured into your lap. For with the measure you use, it will be measured to you." And in Galatians 6:7, "Do not be deceived: God cannot be mocked. A man reaps what he sows." While Luke 6:38 may be perceived as a positive, motivational statement, surely the Galatians 6:7 statement is a factual warning. Both statements articulate the fact that a person gets what they deserve. So Eliphaz stated to Job.

This must have been a shock to Job, that his friend, one of his closest associates who came for the express purpose of comforting him and sharing in his mourning, now, for all practical purposes, accuses Job of some terrible deed or series of deeds so heinous that God has sent this plague to pay him back for his unrighteousness.

The Curse Causeless

Have you ever been falsely accused? Many of us have been. How many times has a person been falsely accused of a crime and had his or her photograph plastered across the newspapers or the Internet, all the while proclaiming their innocence, and even their friends seem to doubt them? Sometimes, these persons are found to be innocent. The same papers and media outlets that announced their supposed guilt rarely (with the same force) proclaim their innocence.

What will we say the next time someone suffers without apparent cause? How will we demonstrate the Christlikeness that God would have us to? How can we comfort those who are dying?

Elder Brown,[2] a staunch Adventist, was dying. He followed a strict vegetarian lifestyle and was a model of health. He was an active Adventist layman, conducting Bible studies and supporting the pastors who passed through the churches in which he participated. Unfortunately, he was eventually stricken with an incurable disease.

When I visited with him in the hospital during his last few days, he mentioned that the physicians had told him he was going to die. I asked him how he felt about dying. He responded that it was all right for him to die; but it wasn't all right for the doctor to live without knowing Jesus. So, he shared his love of Jesus with the doctor.

While he was dying, he pointed someone else to Jesus! An amazing story that is no doubt repeated many times when saints approach their death.

However, Eliphaz had a point, which he presses forth more stridently in chapter 5 of the book of Job. And as pointed out earlier, there is biblical support for his statements. After all, the Bible teaches that the wicked will cease to exist (Psalm 37:10), and in most cases, curses come only because they have a cause-and-effect sense about them (Proverbs 26:2). The problem is, Eliphaz was not about to give Job the benefit of the doubt. In other words, Eliphaz was not willing to "regard someone as innocent until proven otherwise" or to "lean toward a favorable view of someone"[3]—in this case, Job. Since Eliphaz really didn't know why Job was suffering, he could have assumed that Job's protestations were correct and that, as far as Job could know, he hadn't initiated this massive suffering experience by anything he had done.

That is one reason we shouldn't be quick to judge: We don't know everything, even if we think that we do! An old expression comes to mind: "Believe half of what you see and none of what you hear." Our "knowingness" is fallible. Besides that, when we judge, we are often guilty ourselves of something, if not the very thing we are judging others of.

That is what Matthew 7:1, 2 says when it talks about judging, There the word " 'Judge' (*krinō*) can imply *to analyze* or *evaluate* as well as *to condemn* or *avenge*. The former senses are clearly commanded of believers (e.g., 1 Corinthians 5:5; 1 John 4:1), but the latter are reserved for God. Even on those occasions when we render a negative evaluation of others, our purposes should be constructive and not retributive."[4]

Even if Eliphaz had been right, he didn't seem to be constructive, but retributive. He was "right" at the expense of being "loving." And isn't that one of the primary earmarks of being a Christian? "By this shall all men know that you are my disciples, if you have love one to another" (John 13:35, KJ 2000).

Of course, Micah had not yet written his counsel: "He has showed you, O man, what is good; and what does the LORD require of you, but to do justly, and to love mercy, and to walk humbly with your God?" (Micah 6:8, KJ 2000).

These words are easy to read, difficult to live by—for Eliphaz, and for us.

1. Robert L. Alden, *Job,* The New American Commentary, vol. 11 (Nashville, Tenn.: Broadman & Holman, 1993), 69.

2. A pseudonym.

3. *The Free Dictionary,* s.v. "give the benefit of the doubt," http://idioms.thefree dictionary.com/give+the+benefit+of+the+doubt.

4. Craig L. Blomberg, *Matthew,* The New American Commentary, vol. 22 (Nashville, Tenn.: Broadman & Holman, 1992), 127.

CHAPTER 7

Retributive Punishment

In our study of human suffering, the issue or concept of *retributive punishment* arises. *Retributive* is the adjectival form of *retribution*, which, as we know, is a punishment often associated with revenge or vengeance.

Some philosophers theorize that good must punish evil simply because it is the right thing to do, even if there was no other positive outcome from the punishment.

Justice, in its purest form, cannot tolerate evil, and it must not only be addressed—it must be punished. If not, an injustice has occurred.

This idea seems to have some reflection in the reasoning of the three friends of Job, Eliphaz, Bildad, and Zophar, or, in reference to the three of them together, I will call them EBZ.

Remember, Job insisted that he had not sinned. However, the EBZ group, one at a time, insisted with escalating intensity that he must have done something horrendous to undergo this, the apparent just punishment for his unconfessed sins.

Job insisted that his suffering was undeserved because he was not only innocent but also "good."

In some of the biblical presentations dealing with suffering in the world, we struggle with "good" people suffering. We cannot by any means make sense of a baby being stillborn, of people being washed away by a flood, or of a terrorist bombing that kills innocent bystanders.

Of course, this goodness is limited. There are no people who are absolutely good. The Bible is clear on this idea. Consider this inspired statement: "Everyone has turned away, all have become corrupt; there is no one who does good, not even one" (Psalm 53:3). Or take a look at Romans 3:10–12,

> As it is written:
> "There is no one righteous, not even one;
>   there is no one who understands;
>   there is no one who seeks God.
> All have turned away,
>   they have together become worthless;
> there is no one who does good,
>   not even one."

And Jesus spoke these words in Mark 10:18, " 'Why do you call me good?' Jesus answered. 'No one is good—except God alone.' "[1]

God alone is completely good. As human's with fallen natures, even at our best we are still not good in comparison to God. We may compare ourselves to the worst elements in society as the news media portrays them in lurid colors and in graphic details— thinking to ourselves, *I may be bad, but I am not that bad.* It is a practice of comparative righteousness, of which we should beware.

"Men may wrap themselves about with their own righteousness, they may reach their own standard of character, but they do not reach the standard that God has given them in his word. We may measure ourselves by ourselves, and compare ourselves among ourselves; we may say we do as well as this one or as that one, but the great question is, Do we meet the claims that Heaven has upon us?"[2]

God's mercy, compassion, and love allow Him to delay the final retribution on humanity until a date He has set. He does not destroy fallen humanity at this time. In His mercy, He desires to save the entire world and thus leaves time and opportunity for humanity to develop characters that are like His, as far as they can be developed in this world.

However, there are incidents in Scripture that teach us that God does punish sin and evil. EBZ tried mightily to show Job that he fits within the framework of the retributive justice of God.

Job's friends continue in their attempts to reconcile the horrific suffering that Job was enduring with their fallacious idea that each and every bit of suffering was due to the failure of the sufferer to measure up to God's design.

Bildad takes his turn at Job and in essence tells the father of the ten dead children that they died because they were evil, that God does not pervert justice and He killed Job's children because they sinned against Him. In their understanding of God's activity in exercising justice, sinful people got what they deserved. It was like saying to this grieving father, "Your children were wicked, and God took them out. They didn't deserve to live any longer."

There are a few problems with Bildad's reasoning. The first chapter of Job's book demonstrates that Job cared for his children and he actively offered sacrifices to atone for his children in the event that they may have done some unspeakable evil. "For Job said, 'It may be that my sons have sinned and cursed God in their hearts.' Thus Job did regularly" (Job 1:5b, NKJV).

The early record states that he sanctified, or consecrated, his children. Job didn't have a specific, concrete example of sins his children may have committed against God. At least the record doesn't state it. However, he regularly exercised his parental, priestly duty and offered sacrifices on the premise that while feasting or partying, they may have cursed God in their hearts or minds.

Here is a reminder that parents are never truly released from making intercession for their children. When we, by the miracle of procreation, conceive and bring children into the world, our responsibility for their spiritual care never ceases. Job's example may be an extreme one, but at the least we parents should pray for our children, of any age, and remind them of their spiritual calling.

In his speech, Bildad emphasizes one aspect of God's

character—His utter hatred of sin and evil—over any other aspects of His character, especially His merciful disposition towards His children. Bildad was harsh, and sometimes so are we. Once again the author indicates that Bildad, as Eliphaz before him, was trying to defend the character of God at the expense of Job and his children.

I am not so sure that God "needs" us to defend Him. Certainly we are to serve as His witnesses (Isaiah 43:10–12; Acts 1:8), but to argue for God in the absence of God's perspective is a miscarriage of the very justice that Bildad is arguing for.

Let's face it: we only comprehend a little of what God has revealed to us of Himself; and some of what we may understand, we misperceive. One thing is sure; we cannot, now or ever, fully know God's mind.

If we did, He would lose the grandeur of being God.

God's Word produces the balance between law and grace.

"There is perfect harmony between the law of God and the gospel of Jesus Christ. 'I and My Father are one,' says the Great Teacher. The gospel of Christ is the Good News of grace, or favor, by which man may be released from the condemnation of sin and enabled to render obedience to the law of God. The gospel points to the moral code as a rule of life. That law, by its demands for undeviating obedience, is continually pointing the sinner to the gospel for pardon and peace."[3]

There are many who teach that grace covers sin. However, grace, while being clearly defined as "unmerited favor," is more than that. Paul taught Titus: "For the grace of God that brings salvation has appeared to all men, teaching us that, denying ungodliness and worldly lusts, we should live soberly, righteously, and godly in the present age, looking for the blessed hope and glorious appearing of our great God and Savior Jesus Christ, who gave Himself for us, that He might redeem us from every lawless deed and purify for Himself His own special people, zealous for good works" (Titus 2:11–14, NKJV).

As it is written in Job 11:7–9, we cannot search the deep things of God. His motivations are beyond us. They are truly higher than heaven and deeper than Sheol.

Not only do Eliphaz and then Bildad take their respective turn at Job—next we have the third member of the trio of friends, Zophar. EBZ—like a triad of failed, friendly counselors—each take their turn at trying to convince Job that it is his evil that caused his calamitous, torturous experience.

Zophar's turn is found in Job 11:1–20. In summary, Zophar reminds Job that his words need to be responded to when Job claims faultlessness before God (verses 1–4); that he wishes that God would speak and set this man (Job) straight, and that God has forgotten *some* of Job's sins.

Throughout Zophar's presentation is the reminder that God does punish sin.

God directly brought punishment on a world gone wrong by sending the Flood. Simultaneously, God presents his own grace because Noah, while building the ark, preached as he built for 120 years. "A hundred and twenty years before the Flood, the Lord by a holy angel declared to Noah his purpose, and directed him to build an ark. While building the ark he was to preach that God would bring a flood of water upon the earth to destroy the wicked. Those who would believe the message, and would prepare for that event by repentance and reformation, should find pardon and be saved."[4]

While God moved to eradicate the sinful human beings who had taken their sinfulness to levels that His justice could no longer tolerate, he simultaneously provided a way of salvation for those who trusted and believed the warning.

Even while God pronounced the fate of the earth, grace was available for believers. "But Noah found grace in the eyes of the Lord" (Genesis 6:8, NKJV).

And that, my friends, is, as one person said, "just like God." Or to paraphrase another American truism, "That is what He does." While He condemns sin and, in His own way and time, punishes it, God also provides mercy for those who will receive it.

The Flood and Sodom and Gomorrah (Genesis 19) are two examples of God's direct intervention and show His pronouncement against sin and sinners in direct retributive judgment.

While it is very clear that God has taken direct action to

The Book of Job

punish sin and sinners, He also sends a message of promise to those who are willing to obey Him.

In Deuteronomy 6:24, 25, God promises that He will preserve those who seek to "observe all these commands before the LORD our God, as He has commanded us" (NKJV).

In fact the Bible repeatedly reminds us that blessings come as a result of obedience. And all these events were recorded for a blessings to those who live during the ending of this world.

Paul wrote in 1 Corinthians 10:11–13: "Now all these things happened unto them for examples: and they are written for our admonition, upon whom the ends of the ages are come. Therefore let him that thinks he stands take heed lest he fall. There has no temptation taken you but such as is common to man: but God is faithful, who will not allow you to be tempted above that you are able; but will with the temptation also make a way to escape, that you may be able to bear it" (KJ 2000).

It is clear that the records of history are preserved for those who live after the events. As George Santayana said, "Those who do not learn history are doomed to repeat it."

The record of Korah, Dathan, and Abiram in their rebellion against Moses and Aaron is a clear record of retributive justice (Numbers 16). So seriously did God take the challenge of the ringleaders that Moses called on God to do a "new thing"—something altogether different than the Israelites had ever seen before, something that God performed to exonerate not Moses and Aaron but, actually, Himself. This was a direct and awesome display of retributive justice.

Sometimes, people are destroyed because of their own choices: substance abuse takes its toll over the course of years, casual sexual encounters that cause sexually transmitted diseases, and worse.

That is certainly not the case here. The same God whom we refer to as a God of love is also a God of justice, and He is well capable of delivering and will fully demonstrate that aspect of His character at the end of time. He continually calls people to Himself and away from sin. In fact, one aspect of the great controversy is how God will finally eradicate sin from the universe, by cleansing the earth of sin and sinners.

Second Peter 3:5–7 assures that as the Flood took place and destroyed sinners, so in the last day fire will consume the world and destroy those who refuse to follow the Word of God and receive the salvation that Jesus paid for on Calvary.

Malachi states:

> For, behold, the day cometh, that shall burn as an oven; and all the proud, yea, and all that do wickedly, shall be stubble: and the day that cometh shall burn them up, saith the LORD of hosts, that it shall leave them neither root nor branch. But unto you that fear my name shall the Sun of righteousness arise with healing in his wings; and ye shall go forth, and grow up as calves of the stall. And ye shall tread down the wicked; for they shall be ashes under the soles of your feet in the day that I shall do this, saith the LORD of hosts (Malachi 4:1, 2, KJV).

It is clear that the day of retributive judgment is prophesied. However, we are not living in that time yet. We continue to see God's mercy and love being poured out before our very eyes. But one day Jesus will say, "He that is unjust, let him be unjust still: and he which is filthy, let him be filthy still: and he that is righteous, let him be righteous still: and he that is holy, let him be holy still" (Revelation 22:11, KJV).

But until then we continue to heed the admonition of Peter: "But grow in the grace and knowledge of our Lord and Savior Jesus Christ. To him be glory both now and forever! Amen" (2 Peter 3:18).

---

1. Some commentators believe that Jesus' question was designed to elicit the acknowledgment that He was recognized as divine.

2. Ellen G. White, "Jesus Knocking at the Heart," *Signs of the Times*, March 3, 1890, 129, 130.

3. Ellen G. White, *Mind, Character and Personality*, vol. 2 (Hagerstown, Md.: Review and Herald®, 1999), 563.

4. Ellen G. White, *Patriarchs and Prophets* (Mountain View, Calif.: Pacific Press®, 1890, 1913), 92.

CHAPTER 8

Innocent Blood

As we continue our study of the book of Job, we come to a chapter that reveals the deep pain Job was experiencing. In his speech recorded here, we can sense the profound suffering of Job.

While EBZ have expressed themselves quite poetically in their recitation of their theological view, they get some things right and some things wrong. They are correct that God does and will punish sin and sinners. There are some people who are dealt with immediately by the authoritative retributive judgment of the Almighty.

The story of Korah, Dathan, and Abiram, with their dramatic end, reported in Numbers 16 reveals that fact. However, not all suffering and pain is a punishment.

In fact, Job was declared a righteous man—even by God Himself! And that is what is very perplexing to Job; even without knowing what transpired between God and Satan, he staunchly maintained his innocence.

But Job goes even further. He asks God not to condemn him and inquires whether God takes some enjoyment from punishing him (Job 10:3) and despising His own creation. He asks God to reveal his sin because this poor man is unaware of anything that he may have thought, said, or done that would result in this type of treatment.

Unfortunately, our "hero" Job attributes everything that is happening to the hand of God, whom he has served faithfully.

Again and again, readers of this epic tale are reminded that we have the advantage of knowing how and why it started and how it ends. But in the midst of it all, Job is left to his own imagination, thoughts, and ponderings along with the nearly convincing presentations of his friends.

What do we do with our friends like them? Do you have any friends like Eliphaz, Bildad, and Zophar? I hope not!

Through it all, Job maintained his integrity, refusing to "curse God and die" as his wife admonished him to do.

Thus far, we do not have the answer we are looking for. While Job's suffering was perhaps a pinnacle experience, we do not have the answer, or at least Job doesn't have the answer, to his unique suffering. And remember, Job is not just suffering the physical pain. Oh, it must have been extreme, but he also suffered the social stigma articulated by his close friends, which probably was the talk of the town. *Possessions gone, children and servants killed, body racked by an incurable disease, what did he do to deserve* that? the townspeople must have thought.

Primarily, Job was suffering because God knew Job and Job knew God. According to God, Job was more fit to represent the earth in the heavenly council gatherings than was Satan. God knew that He could depend on Job to represent Him and the values of His kingdom.

But what would we say to Job if on scene with him and watching him suffer? What do we say to our fellow church members, our neighbors, our work associates when an incurable disease strikes? I have learned that platitudes don't help when people suffer—at any level.

A relative told me about a sermon on disappointment, suffering, and pain in which the pastor admonished his parishioners to "build a bridge and get over it!" Talk about insensitivity! That is no better than, "Deal with it!" or "This too shall pass," or "Don't give up; God is on your side." Sometimes the silence of God makes the pain of suffering almost unbearable.

Besides being insensitive, the approach of giving trite

platitudes is insufficient on any level to help people with their suffering. And just as Job was undeserving of his unearned sufferings, many people today suffer unjustly—for example, the young woman who is attacked and savagely brutalized while she is walking home.

Between 2002 and 2004, three young women, Michelle Knight, Amanda Berry, and Georgina "Gina" DeJesus, were kidnapped by Ariel Castro (July 10, 1960–September 3, 2013) in his home in the Tremont neighborhood of Cleveland, Ohio. They were subsequently imprisoned in his house on Seymour Avenue until May 6, 2013, when Berry escaped with her six-year-old daughter and contacted the police. Knight and DeJesus were rescued by responding officers, and Castro was arrested within hours.

These three women suffered the cruel fate of being sexually tortured during their imprisonment. They didn't deserve what they got. They and the millions of others who are victims of sexual abuse in our world today do not deserve the suffering that is perpetrated upon them.

And yet, we are more than aware of the biblical teachings on the evil of corruption of the human heart and man's inhumanity to man. Sin has touched us all. In fact, the Bible records Solomon's prayer at the opening of the temple he had constructed. In his prayer he said, "When they sin against you—for there is no one who does not sin" (1 Kings 8:46). What an acknowledgement. No one is free from sin. No one.

Gradually, through the direct guidance of God, we are brought to the place of acknowledging our own fallen state. Our thoughts, our words, and our actions, tainted with selfishness, make any sincere Christian cry out like Paul did, "O wretched man that I am! who shall deliver me from the body of this death? I thank God through Jesus Christ our Lord. So then with the mind I myself serve the law of God; but with the flesh the law of sin" (Romans, 7:24, 25, KJV).

"But Satan's aim has been to lead men to self first; and yielding themselves to his control, they have developed a selfishness that has filled the world with misery and strife, setting human beings at variance with one another."[1]

"All sin is selfishness. Satan's first sin was selfishness. He sought to grasp power, to exalt self. A species of insanity led him to seek to supersede God. And the temptation which led Adam to sin, was the false statement of Satan that it was possible for him to attain to something more than he already enjoyed—possible for him to be as God Himself. Thus seeds of selfishness were sown in the human heart."[2]

To break the hold of self on our hearts, we need the Lord of the Cross, Jesus the righteous Son of God. "The sacrifice of Christ as an atonement for sin is the great truth around which all other truths cluster. In order to be rightly understood and appreciated, every truth in the word of God, from Genesis to Revelation, must be studied in the light that streams from the cross of Calvary. I present before you the great, grand monument of mercy and regeneration, salvation and redemption—the Son of God uplifted on the cross."[3]

But Job and his friends obviously had no New Testament to point them to Christ's great sacrifice that would one day eliminate all selfishness and resulting sin from the world, as we do.

There are some examples, of course, where people suffer with no apparent connection to known sin. The disciples in their day also suffered from the commonly held belief that all sin was due to the sinfulness of the sufferer. But Jesus demonstrated that this is not always the case. In John 9:1–5 we find the following:

As he went along, he saw a man blind from birth. His disciples asked him, "Rabbi, who sinned, this man or his parents, that he was born blind?"

"Neither this man nor his parents sinned," said Jesus, "but this happened so that the works of God might be displayed in him. As long as it is day, we must do the works of him who sent me. Night is coming, when no one can work. While I am in the world, I am the light of the world."

After this statement, Jesus healed the blind man in a most

unusual manner. He spat on the ground, made mud from the dirt and His saliva, applied it to the man's eyes, and instructed him to go and wash in the Pool of Siloam. The blind man was healed from his blindness. Of course there is more to the story, but we cannot elaborate on it at this juncture.

In Job 15:14–16, Eliphaz refocuses on human sinfulness by reminding Job that there is no man that is pure. Sometimes we say that suffering purifies the vision and clarifies the goal. Sometimes we acknowledge that the suffering God allows to come into our lives is to remove the "dross" from our lives—that the purity of the true godly character, like gold under the refiner's fire, may be revealed.[4] Many times we can trace no benefit or goodness from the suffering that people endure. And while suffering, some people turn away from God, which is one of Satan's goals in using pain and suffering.

There is so much evil in the world that it is more than a challenge to see any good that comes from it. And we cannot defend it at all. We can't perfectly understand it, either. But we can choose to suspend our final judgment on these acts of suffering and the God who seemingly allows them to happen.

There are hard questions to be answered. Maybe we need to say what Abraham said when he bargained with God over the destruction of Sodom and Gomorrah: "Far be it from you to do such a thing—to kill the righteous with the wicked, treating the righteous and the wicked alike. Far be it from you! Will not the Judge of all the earth do right?" (Genesis 18:25).

Countless scriptural references speak to the fact that we should not "borrow" trouble from the future and also remind us that life in this world will never be fair: Job's family was destroyed (Job 1:18–20); righteous Abel was killed by his brother (Genesis 4:8); David conspired to kill Uriah the Hittite to cover his adultery (2 Samuel 11); Jeremiah was imprisoned in a muddy dungeon for delivering the word of the Lord (Jeremiah 32:2, 3); John the Baptist was beheaded for calling sin by its right name (Matthew 14:10); and an unnamed host of faithful people were mocked, tortured, imprisoned, and worse for their faith in God's only begotten Son.

Since the Bible acknowledges suffering and pain in this

present world, it is unwise for God's followers to think that they will be exempt in this life from any and all forms of suffering. In fact, Jesus states that we shouldn't worry about tomorrow's problems, "borrowing" them from the future.

Commenting on Matthew 6:34, the culmination of a sermon Jesus gave to instruct his followers on meeting the issues of life, The New American Commentary states: "Again, Jesus uses the characteristically Jewish type of reasoning—from the lesser to the greater. If the logic of his argument be granted, then worry can only result from a lack of genuine belief in God's goodness and mercy. R. Mounce says, 'Worry is practical atheism and an affront to God.' "[5]

Wow—strong words!

The *Seventh-day Adventist Bible Commentary* on the same passage, Matthew 6:34, states:

> Christians can be free from anxiety in the midst of the most distressing circumstances, fully assured that He who does everything well (cf. Mark 7:37) will make all things "work together for good" (Romans 8:28). God knows all about tomorrow; we know not "what a day may bring forth" (Proverbs 27:1). And He who knows all about tomorrow bids us to trust in His continued watchcare and to "take . . . no [anxious] thought" concerning its problems and perplexities. When tomorrow comes, its anticipated troubles often prove to have been wholly imaginary. Too many people permit themselves to be haunted by the ghost of tomorrow before tomorrow ever comes.[6]

As we focus on Jesus' teaching, we find that He acknowledged the seeming capriciousness of life with its unfairness and evil suffering. He experienced it himself: at the announcement of His birth, Herod slaughtered unnumbered male babies in an attempt to remove a competitor to the throne (Matthew 2:16–18); and His trial was a mockery of justice, with witnesses who perjured themselves. Finally, He was nailed to the cross that He was forced to carry, and this after Pilate had announced three times, "I find no fault in Him!" (John 18:38, 19:4, 6). Talk about unfair and unjust! Jesus experienced all of that for us.

Unwittingly, Job was a type of Christ, suffering unjustly. And Satan attacked him, just as he attacked Christ.

Job's situation is not the standard for suffering—if there is such a thing. But in his example we see faithfulness in the midst of unjust suffering.

While the Bible never teaches that people will be free from pain and suffering in this world, it does give us hope.

I used to be an avid racquetball player. When one of my opponents gained a rare advantage in the match against me, he would say: "Hope is a terrible thing to give a man." Meaning, of course, that hope brings an intangible benefit. We have hope that this world will soon pass away at the coming of the Lord, and then there will be established a new order of things, a new type of living, if you please.

And throughout Scripture we find hope for the inhabitants of this sin-filled and evil-saturated world. While pain and suffering abound, so does hope. Maybe that's why Proverbs recommends that we "trust in the LORD with all thine heart; and lean not unto thine own understanding. In all thy ways acknowledge him, and he shall direct thy paths" (Proverbs 3:5, 6, KJV).

In spite of what we know intellectually or what we cannot figure out in our own trained intellect, we are called to trust in the Lord. Trust in God is an easy thing to articulate when we are doing fine. But to really experience trust or faith when things go wrong is another thing. With each problem or struggle, suffering or difficulty, we should, as Christians, trust in the goodness of God—not because we feel like it, but because we know it is true.

The song our children learn in Sabbath School has it right: "Jesus loves me! this I know, for the Bible tells me so." Because the Bible makes it plain, we accept it in faith.

This is what Job expressed when he proclaimed, "Though He slay me, yet will I trust in Him" (Job 13:15, KJV).

---

1. Ellen G. White, *Counsels on Stewardship* (Takoma Park, Md.: Review and Herald®, 1940), 24.

2. Ellen G. White, "To Brn-Srs. of the Iowa Conference (cf. Lt 134, 1902)," *The Ellen G. White 1888 Materials*, 1763.

3. Ellen G. White, *Gospel Workers* (Takoma Park, Md.: Review and Herald®, 1915), 315.

4. See White, *Patriarchs and Prophets*, 129.

5. Blomberg, *Matthew*, vol. 22, 125, 126.

6. Nichol, *The Seventh-day Adventist Bible Commentary*, 2nd ed., vol. 5, 353.

Intimations of Hope

As we have been studying the book of Job, we are brought to a spot of hope. This hope is expressed strongly as Job replies to his friends.

The Bible tells us not to put our trust or hope in another person, because those people cannot save. In fact other human beings are of the same nature as us: flesh is temporary and will pass into the grave. But the person who is blessed is the one who puts their trust in the Lord.

Nor can we invest trust in organizations because, in a sense, human-led organizations are, perhaps unwittingly, a combination of the traits of those who comprise them, and at their best they are still fallible. No, it is best to follow the recommendations of the Bible:

> Do not put your trust in princes,
>   in human beings, who cannot save.
> When their spirit departs, they return to the ground;
>   on that very day their plans come to nothing.
> Blessed are those whose help is the God of Jacob,
>   whose hope is in the LORD their God (Psalm 146:3–5).

Job's hope certainly was located in God, His Savior.

Job's friends, the EBZ group, had pushed hard at him to get him to admit the specifics of his horrible sin. Remember, they are still caught in the grip of the fallacious idea that all suffering is the direct result of God's divine retribution.

We don't need the Bible to remind us that we are living in a wicked world. We can just mention a few words, names of infamous people and places, and instantly our minds are taken to places of horror recorded in history: Adolf Hitler, Auschwitz, Rwanda, Kosovo. We can think of events of nature: hurricanes, tsunamis, earthquakes—and the list goes on and on.

What we have come to realize is that this world is a wicked place and the enemy of God is free to influence and control much of what happens here.

Job's friends had, by their consistent and persistent accusations, actually joined the enemy in bringing words that would discourage most people. Their tactlessness and lack of compassion had mischaracterized Job—and the God they sought to defend. And Job has had it. He isn't going to take it anymore; he decides that enough is enough.

Should we be prepared to defend ourselves against false accusations? Absolutely. Jesus is our example in all things. He remained mute when falsely accused, (Isaiah 53:7), likely because of his divinely appointed role as our Savior to bear the sins and burdens of all humanity. He took our guilt joyfully and wore our shame on the cross.

Jesus did enter into dialogue to defend himself with His critics prior to entering into His passion (see Luke 5:17–26 and Matthew 12:1–8). But after Gethsemane, Jesus no longer responded to His critics and accusers from a position of defense. He came to fulfill a unique role that we are not called to fulfill.

Job was undergoing a severe test and trial; in the same way, all of us will be tested. Why the test? Remember, God knew the intent of Job's heart. But Satan and the rest of the angels—the holy ones as well as the evil ones—did not.

Job had been accounted blameless, upright, God-fearing, and eschewing evil. Now he is being put to the test, not for the benefit of God but for the witnesses—the heavenly beings who were watching the great controversy being played out before their very eyes. The "sons of God" who had heard Satan's accusation were watching to see whether it was possible for humans to be faithful to God—for faith to sustain through severe trials and tribulation, as God knew it to be possible.

"Hope and courage are essential to perfect service for God. These are the fruit of faith. Despondency is sinful and unreasonable. God is able and willing 'more abundantly' (Hebrews 6:17) to bestow upon His servants the strength they need for test and trial. The plans of the enemies of His work may seem to be well laid and firmly established, but God can overthrow the strongest of these. And this He does in His own time and way, when He sees that the faith of His servants has been sufficiently tested."[1]

Job's hope was in the Lord. And, despite all that came his way, he maintained his faith in God. Paul explains to us that hope is a by-product of faith: "Therefore, having been justified by faith, we have peace with God through our Lord Jesus Christ, through whom also we have access by faith into this grace in which we stand, and rejoice in hope of the glory of God. And not only that, but we also glory in tribulations, knowing that tribulation produces perseverance; and perseverance, character; and character, hope. Now hope does not disappoint, because the love of God has been poured out in our hearts by the Holy Spirit who was given to us" (Romans 5:1–5, NKJV).

Did you catch it? Paul says that tribulations produce perseverance; perseverance develops character; and character, hope. And hope doesn't disappoint us! It rewards us. But Job, of course, didn't have Paul's or any Bible writings to help him understand what was happening. He did have hope because he had faith in God. That sustained him through his horrific trial.

James the apostle addresses this in his general epistle. He says, "Consider it pure joy, my brothers and sisters, whenever you face trials of many kinds, because you know that the testing of your faith produces perseverance" (James 1:2, 3). James tells us that we should consider it, or think it, a joy when trials and troubles and tribulations come upon us.

"It is the privilege and duty of the Christian to take an

intelligent attitude toward the tests and trials that beset his pathway. He needs to study and understand God's permissive relationship to such experiences."[2] When trials, troubles, and tribulations come, we must give thought to see how they fit into God's program. I can hear some of you saying, "It is easier said than done." And it is. But that is what God is working out in us the — progressive development of refined characters.

We need to remember what Paul said: "And we know that *all* things work together for good to them that love God, to them who are the called according to his purpose" (Romans 8:28, KJV; emphasis added).

Obviously, not everything that happens to us is good. A body racked with cancer, AIDS, or a paralytic stroke is not good. Neither heart attacks nor bankruptcy is good. Neither is divorce or domestic violence. And the list could go on and on. But God uses these things as His tools to perfect the character of His children.

Knowing that God permits trials, troubles, and tribulations to come our way for our eventual perfection should let us know that God is still at work in our lives. When we realize that fact, perhaps then we can "count it all joy." Only the mature or growing Christian can have this attitude. We can expect these trials, troubles, and tribulations and receive them with a spiritual joy; but it is indeed a challenge. Jesus, confronted with the cross, was able to look beyond His sufferings to the salvation of the human race (see Hebrews 12:2). The joy is not that we are experiencing the trials, but it is because we are aware of the end result of the trial.

The devil uses the trials to tempt us to sin or just to harass us. He brings us these trials in an attempt to break our focus on God. It is, however, his goal to go beyond harassment and temptation; he wants us to lose faith in Jesus completely. Our heavenly Father, however, in His permissive will, allows the devil to annoy, harass, and trouble us. The Father allows the "ministry of suffering and temptation"[3] for the formation of character.

Character is what we are. In Christ, each stumbling block that the devil throws in our path can become a stepping-stone to salvation. During each trial, trouble, or tribulation that we experience, we may have the assurance that the proving that takes place grows our faith in God. Our faith must be mature in order for us to enter into God's eternal kingdom. Our faith must be undaunted, uncompromising. Our faith must be tested and tried. This faith is the utter confidence that Jesus Christ has the best plan for our lives. When we have a faith that has passed all the tests, we realize that nothing and no one can hinder the plan God has for His children. Job never lost faith in God, even though he did not understand why he was going through his trials (see Job 1:20–22; 2:7–10).

Under the pressure of his friends' accusations, Job sought an audience with God. He wanted answers to his questions, and he declares that he wants to reason with God. Job knows deep in his heart that he is innocent of all these charges, and in seeking to defend himself, he resorts to appeal beyond this "court" composed of Eliphaz, Bildad, and Zophar, who had already judged him guilty.

In essence, Job appeals to a higher authority. And it is interesting that through Isaiah the prophet, God invites us to reason with Him. "Come now, and let us reason together, saith the LORD: though your sins be as scarlet, they shall be as white as snow; though they be red like crimson, they shall be as wool" (Isaiah 1:18, KJV).

God is not beyond dialogue and reasoning with His people. And in seeking vindication, Job goes to the Supreme Court of the Universe, as it were. He wants to go to the final authority. Job went so far as to acknowledge that God was responsible for his suffering, and yet in the midst of it he states, "Though he slay me, yet will I trust in him: but I will maintain mine own ways before him" (Job 13:15, KJV).

I once heard Dr. Leslie Pollard, president of Oakwood University, preach a sermon about David when he faced down Goliath in the valley of Elah. Pollard said that David "downloaded his resume" when preparing for the historic battle. By that, he meant that David remembered how he had been victorious over a bear and a lion in "hand to paw" combat and prevailed. In short, remember the battles God brought you through in the past.

Whatever difficulties and trials God has seen us through or given us victory over remind us of His presence and His promise (see Hebrews 13:5) and assure us of His presence in the present and future because "Jesus Christ is the same yesterday, today and forever" (Hebrews 13:8).

Job must have had some previous experience with God that enabled him to say with such force, "Though He slay me, yet will I trust Him." Under the attack of an unknown foe and with no support from his closest friends; apparently abandoned by his community, Job could have descended into a deep, dark hole of despair—permanently. He had a choice, as do we all, how we respond to what Satan throws at us. What a marvelous testimony! Trusting God while undergoing an undeserved attack on life and limb is superlative!

Ellen White further states, "From the depths of discouragement and despondency Job rose to the heights of implicit trust in the mercy and the saving power of God. Triumphantly he declared: 'Though He slay me, yet will I trust in Him.' "[4]

Reading across the centuries, one gets the impression that Job had no rational reason for the hope that lay within him. But he must have had an experience with God to allow this hope in the Lord to vindicate him. Job also had a hope in the resurrection. He looked, by faith, beyond his present situation to the day of the resurrection.

Once again, Job did not have any biblical information on which to base his expectations; the hope he had in God allowed him to look forward to a resurrection, the great hope of the church in all ages. This hope exists because of the fact that Jesus rose victoriously from the grave, leaving death empty-handed.

Ephesians 1:4 and Titus 1:2 both join other Bible passages to remind us that God chose us before the Creation of the world and that God, who cannot lie, promised before time began that He would bestow on faithful humans eternal life. Amazing thought—that God, who knows the capacity of free moral agents to choose to sin or obey, still created us!

In Genesis 22, we have the story of Abraham's test regarding his complete loyalty to God by following the command of God to sacrifice his son Isaac by killing him and offering him as a burnt offering. I cannot imagine being in Abraham's place. He had wanted this child for so long, and God had promised and restated the promise to Abraham and Sarah that they would be parents. In addition, the command to sacrifice Isaac went absolutely contrary to all he knew about Jehovah God.

When Isaac approached the site of the sacrifice, he inquired about the whereabouts of the lamb. His father responded by saying, "The Lord Himself will provide the lamb for a burnt offering." As Abraham raised the knife to strike the bound Isaac in the chest, the Angel of the Lord[5] stopped him, and Abraham found a ram in the thicket. Jehovah had indeed provided a sacrifice for the offering.

"And Abraham called the name of that place Jehovah-jireh: as it is said to this day, In the mount of the Lord it shall be seen" (Genesis 22:14, KJV).

YHWH-Yireh, or *Jehovah-jireh,* which means "the Lord will provide."

Job had the conviction that even though he was going through a torturous experience, God would see him through.

Let's go back to a verse we looked at earlier, Romans 5:3–5: "Not only so, but we also glory in our sufferings, because we know that suffering produces perseverance; perseverance, character; and character, hope. *And hope does not put us to shame,* because God's love has been poured out into our hearts through the Holy Spirit, who has been given to us" (emphasis added).

Hope does not result in shame because of the focus of the hope. We have hope in Jesus, our Savior. Job had hope in his Redeemer. Hope was his anchor, and it held fast through the storm he went through.

"And the peace of God, which transcends all understanding, will guard your hearts and your minds in Christ Jesus" (Philippians 4:7). That is, our hope also brings us into a peace beyond our ability to understand. We know that the Lord will provide whatever we need to be faithful and to be victorious in His name.

That was Job's hope. How about ours?

1. White, *Prophets and Kings*, 164.
2. Nichol, *Seventh-day Adventist Bible Commentary*, vol. 7, 503.
3. Nichol, *Seventh-day Adventist Bible Commentary*, vol. 7, 504.
4. White, *Prophets and Kings*, 163, 164.
5. Many believe this to be a reference to a preincarnate appearance of Jesus.

CHAPTER

10

The Wrath of Elihu

Have you ever been filled with wrath? That word is foreign to the daily vocabulary of the twenty-first century. My electronic dictionary defines *wrath* as "extreme anger."

It is safe to say that we all have been angry at something or someone at some time. We may have even experienced extreme anger over something or at someone.

Anger is not forbidden or sinful; after all, Ephesians 4:26 says, "Be angry, and sin not: let not the sun go down upon your wrath" (KJ 2000).

In other words, it is possible and maybe even commendable to be angry without sinning, but the limits to our anger or wrath, in terms of a time context, is confined to the end of the day. This suggests that people should seek to resolve the issues that cause their anger and not let it "fester" in the subconscious overnight while we sleep.

So in our story, Elihu shows up, and he is *extremely angry,* or wrathful. Let's take a look at what is going on that makes him so angry.

During the bulk of the book of Job, the argument between Job and his buddies continues. Back and forth they go, each one attempting to justify his beliefs and himself with rhetoric and logical reasoning. It is really an unfair competition—three against one. And it gets worse.

During the dialogue, however, some pretty important truths are presented that cannot be ignored: "So man wastes away like something rotten, like a garment eaten by moths" (Job 13:28). It is a fact that our bodies, under the effects of sin, just wear out. Adam and Eve were built to last. That ended when sin began. They lived a long time; according to Scripture, Adam died at 930 years of age. Amazing, but he still died. My wife's grandmother, Mrs. Mattie Black, is 99 years old. Next year, if the Lord is willing, we will celebrate her 100th birthday. What a wonderful thing. We celebrate when people reach the century mark. But God's original plan was that we would live forever.

Many people who reach a certain age develop physical ailments—sometimes more than one. And all the people we know will die. Death and dying are part of this world until Jesus comes. We decay, we wear out, and we die. Our present bodies are not built for eternity. That is one reason why we are told in the New Testament: "So when this corruptible shall have put on incorruption, and this mortal shall have put on immortality, then shall be brought to pass the saying that is written, Death is swallowed up in victory. O death, where is thy sting? O grave, where is thy victory? The sting of death is sin; and the strength of sin is the law. But thanks be to God, which giveth us the victory through our Lord Jesus Christ" (1 Corinthians 15:54–57, KJV).

The above transition from corruptible to incorruptible and mortal to immortal is necessitated because fallen flesh cannot "inherit" the kingdom of God (1 Corinthians 15:50). The impurity of the natural man makes us incompatible with God's holy nature. We need the new birth that Jesus described to Nicodemus: "Very truly I tell you, no one can see the kingdom of God unless they are born again" (John 3:3).

We need both the physical and the spiritual renewal—or rebirth—that only God can provide. First the spiritual, then the physical restoration will come as God keeps His promise. After all, He is the original promise maker and promise keeper. Job knew that he would die and be devoured by worms, but with conviction he stated his belief that he would see his Redeemer, and that Redeemer is Jesus Christ (Job 19:25–27).

Perhaps Job reached beyond his education in order to be informed by his faith. He echoed the faith stated in the words of Paul in 2 Corinthians 4:16–18, "Therefore we do not lose heart. Though outwardly we are wasting away, yet inwardly we are being renewed day by day. For our light and momentary troubles are achieving for us an eternal glory that far outweighs them all. So we fix our eyes not on what is seen, but on what is unseen, since what is seen is temporary, but what is unseen is eternal."

By faith, Job understood that death is not a "period" at the end of life; it is not the end—it is but a comma for those who love God.

Jesus made it clear that only the pure in heart would see God (Matthew 5:8). Job, blameless, upright, God-fearing, and avoiding evil, must have had a pure heart. He also defines or equates wisdom with fearing or respecting God. That is why David wrote, "The fool has said in his heart, there is no God" (Psalms 14:1; 53:1, NKJV).

As has been pointed out, all of the speakers in the narrative are limited in their application of their principles because they all have partial knowledge. All of us "see through a glass, darkly" (1 Corinthians 13:12, KJV). New technology brings a rapid increase of information. And, while information may be used to increase one's knowledge base, no one knows everything—if only because information on all subjects continues to grow daily.

We only know what God has revealed about Himself. And as stated elsewhere, God hasn't told us everything about Himself and His ways. Thus, we should speak about the deep things of God with humility, recognizing that the "secret things belong to . . . God" (Deuteronomy 29:29).

Now, in Job 32:1–5, the EBZ group, perhaps out of a sense of frustration, ended their debate with Job because he was "righteous in his own eyes." And then Elihu shows up. *Elihu* means, "He is my God." Where has this brother been? Perhaps he came later, or maybe he was there all the time. It appears that he was listening and thinking and judging the dialogue between Job and the EBZ group. Apparently, he must have been a friend of the others or maybe an associate of Job. He speaks last because the others were his elders; he showed respect and waited his turn.

But he is an angry young man; his anger being aroused is mentioned four times. And his anger is specific. He became displeased as he listened to the elders and Job—at least in part because Job continually sought to vindicate himself. He would not "own" what the others had told him repeatedly with reasoning from their point of view that he had to be a gross sinner to have received this type of punishment—divine retribution— directly from the hand of God. Also, he criticized EBZ because they had not presented a cogent, satisfactory answer to Job's defensive argument. He reasoned that both sides were misrepresenting God.

Was Elihu's anger justified? Was it what we would call "righteous indignation"? Righteous indignation is anger stimulated by injustice or misrepresentation. It is usually objective; it is not usually about self or selfish interests. When we are angry with God's misrepresentation, that is righteous indignation. Jesus displayed righteous indignation over the misrepresentation of His Father's house (see Luke 19:46). His example is always appropriate to follow.

However, we should think carefully before we display our anger. Time and place and choice of words are always things we need to think about when we speak critically. Nevertheless, Elihu makes several good points that still stand true today:

First, God cannot do wrong (Job 34:10). It is a fact that God only does what is holy, righteous, and pure.

Second, God will not wrongly punish people. He is just and will reward people based on their works (Revelation 22:12).

Third, God can destroy all life on earth at once, if He so chooses.

The problem with Elihu's argument is not found in the points he makes but in the assumption, without any evidence whatsoever, that Job was guilty of sin.

However, what is glaringly absent from all arguments presented in the defense of God is a reflection or presentation of God's compassion:

The enemy of good blinded the minds of men, so that they looked upon God with fear; they thought of Him as severe and unforgiving. Satan led men to conceive of God as a being whose chief attribute is stern justice,—one who is a severe judge, a harsh, exacting creditor. He pictured the Creator as a being who is watching with jealous eye to discern the errors and mistakes of men, that He may visit judgments upon them. It was to remove this dark shadow, by revealing to the world the infinite love of God, that Jesus came to live among men. . . .

. . . Love, mercy, and compassion were revealed in every act of [Jesus'] life; His heart went out in tender sympathy to the children of men. . . .

Jesus did not suppress one word of truth, but He uttered it always in love. He exercised the greatest tact and thoughtful, kind attention in His intercourse with the people. He was never rude, never needlessly spoke a severe word, never gave needless pain to a sensitive soul. He did not censure human weakness. He spoke the truth, but always in love. He denounced hypocrisy, unbelief, and iniquity; but tears were in His voice as He uttered His scathing rebukes. . . .

Such is the character of Christ as revealed in His life. This is the character of God. It is from the Father's heart that the streams of divine compassion, manifest in Christ, flow out to the children of men. Jesus, the tender, pitying Saviour, was God "manifest in the flesh" (1 Timothy 3:16).[1]

It really seems a misrepresentation of God's character to harshly judge people, even in sin, without demonstrating compassion.

Perhaps we think that to be compassionate with people is to condone their sin. Maybe we don't want to be considered "soft" on sin, recognizing the need to call sin by its right name. While it is correct to do so, we must ask ourselves whether we invalidate God's process when we are harsh and condemning of others, realizing that we do not know all the details as only God can. I wish that I got it right all the time; Jesus, our example, demonstrated the correct balance of speaking truth to evil without condemning evildoers. But I, as we all are, am a work in progress.

It is clear that Job's friends focused only on God's justice; however, they failed to capture His entire nature. It may be because they had never had the total experience with God for themselves. When we contemplate evil and the presence of sin, we really have to remember that it is a mysterious irrationality.

Paul calls it the "mystery of iniquity" (2 Thessalonians 2:7). A mystery is a deep secret. While we can read about the fall of Lucifer and his transition to Satan, we cannot logically explain why he chose to sin and rebel. We can explain it but maybe not to our total understanding. It is nonsensical to choose a path of self-destruction that has wrecked the world, as it were.

The practice of sin and evil result in so much deep pain and loss; it is irrational for us to choose it—yet the pleasures of sin seem so enticing that we humans often choose it rather than growth-causing faithful obedience.

And yet that is what happened (see Ezekiel 28:12–17).

We see that Job's friends, and Elihu, failed to include the activity of Satan, the devil, in their reasoning. How could they? They didn't know that everything that came upon Job—all his suffering—was *not* his fault but the result of Satan's attempt to prove God and Job to be false. Satan failed miserably because Job, though truly an innocent bystander, maintained his faith in God. I have often likened faith to the currency of Heaven. God answers our faith; He honors it.

Whenever we read the miraculous works of Jesus, we almost always find someone having their faith mentioned in the story. Matthew 9:18–30 records three events in rapid succession that reveal the importance of our faith: the woman with the hemorrhage, the raising of the synagogue ruler's daughter, and the restoration of sight for two blind men.

The attack on Job can be viewed as an attack on his faith. Our faith, as Job's was, is a powerful tool in the battle of holiness. God always rewards our faith in Him. That may be why 1 John 5:4 states: "For whatsoever is born of God overcometh the world: and this is the victory that overcometh the world, even our faith" (KJV).

Satan recognizes the importance of our faith, knowing that the correct operation of faith—trusting God completely—leads to his defeat. While Satan attacked Job for no reason except that God pointed him out as more worthy to represent the earth in the council meeting, God answered Job's faith.

And He always answers ours too.

------

1. White, *Steps to Christ,* 10–12.

CHAPTER 11

Out of the Whirlwind

The thirty-eighth chapter of Job answers some questions but raises several others: Heretofore, one could have asked, Where is God? Does God hear? Does God answer? As one man exclaimed while examining the trouble and evil in the world: "Where is God? I want to tell Him something!"

Why is it that we believe in talking to God (prayer), but when someone says that God spoke back, we doubt their sanity, intelligence, or sincerity?

Job had the experience of speaking to God and speaking about God for a protracted period of time. In his tale, not only does God not speak to Job's uncompassionate friends—his "miserable comforters"—but Job also continually cries out to God and even asks for an audience with the Almighty.

To be sure, he is not the only one in Scripture who called out to God and received no answer. But how about us? Do we cry out and expect an answer? Did Job, or was he speaking rhetorically?

In any event, God answered. And boy, *did* He answer.

After the dialogue between Job, the EBZ group, and Elihu, God finally speaks to Job, but he ignores the others altogether.

And God speaks during the storm. What should we do when God speaks? Listen. What should we do when God speaks from the storm—the whirlwind? Listen intently.

But this is not the only time God has spoken to human beings; He has done so since the beginning of time. He spoke with Adam and Eve in the Garden of Eden, and the first recorded dialogue between God and man was God's question, "Where are you?" (Genesis 3:9, NKJV). God wasn't asking about Adam and Eve's geographical location—as Creator, He certainly knew that. He was inquiring about the change in the status of their relationship to Him. They were hiding, and man was created, not to hide from God, but to have intimacy with God.

God is concerned about our relationship to Him, which is why He promised to send someone to stand between the seed of the serpent and the seed of the woman (Genesis 3:15). That is exactly why God sent his Son to die—to ransom guilty humanity from the clutches of the evil usurper and enemy, Satan—and restore us to the oneness He longs to have with us. He is ever seeking to redeem, to save, to forgive, and to inspire to righteous living.

And when He speaks to Job, He is not supplying simple statements to answer Job's questions; His rhetorical questions may have been the model for the Socratic method of teaching—which, perhaps over-simplistically stated, is the art of asking critical questions designed to prompt deep thought.

The very first question God asks Job is one of identification: "Who is this who darkens counsel by words without knowledge?" (Job 38:2, NKJV). What a question! To have God state that our conversation darkens rather than illuminates is a humbling experience indeed. This question was evaluative in nature. That is, the question itself reveals the value that the Questioner finds in the collective statements of the person being addressed: Job.

God's questions were actually a rebuke to Job. For, as we examine the statements of Job, we find that even though he was "blameless," he had misrepresented God.

"For Job to suggest that God had become his enemy would only confuse others about God rather than shed light on His ways. Because of this Job . . . did not really know whereof he spoke when he blamed God for being unfair. Job's words were without knowledge (as Elihu had twice said; 34:35; 35:16)."[1]

How often could our speech or conversation be classified as "without knowledge"?

Sometimes, we speak inadvisably and reveal our ignorance, or lack of knowledge. However, God not only enlightens Job to his own limited knowledge but also points to the Questioner, God Himself, as the ultimate answer.

Several years ago while I conducted a local church business meeting, one of the members offered a suggested answer to our shared challenge. While I cannot remember the problem or the answer, I do remember that her answer caused a snicker to roll through the gathering of the small congregation. I fought the urge to smile, because I knew that if I did, others might laugh, and I wanted to show respect to this senior saint. For a brief moment, all eyes were on me. Everyone was waiting for my response. I said, "Sister, I certainly appreciate your zeal for the Lord." She then said, "Yes, pastor, but it is without knowledge, isn't it?" At which we all had a good laugh, including our sister.

Many times, God reveals Himself through dialogue.

He spoke intimately with Abram (Genesis 15:1–6) when the latter painfully recognized he had no heir—no one to carry on his bloodline, no one to carry his name into the future. God spoke to Abram and assured him that his heartfelt desire for a son would be answered in the affirmative, not by human devising but by God keeping His promise through Sarai. This demonstrates, as in many other cases, that God cares about the cares of humanity. What we are concerned with is important to God too.

Jacob wrestled with a Man all night until the breaking of the dawn, asked a blessing, and received a new name. He talked with the Man who was Jesus in a theophany, a preincarnation appearance of God in flesh (see Genesis 32:22–30).

In fact, God asked Job a series of questions—beginning with telling him, in essence, to get ready, brace himself, prepare himself: here comes true knowledge. "Prepare yourself like a man; I will question you, and you shall answer Me" (Job 38:3, NKJV). How would you and I respond to that?

He then asks Job where he was at the Creation. As God revealed His creative power to Job by this series of questions, Job was being educated about the grandeur, the utter awesomeness of who God is, by focusing on what God has done.

With the advance of science, humanity may be able to answer some of the questions that God asks in chapters 38 and 39, but mostly we will have to say, "I don't know." With all due respect to the work of dedicated scientists, there still exists much more that is unknown to us in every field of study.

And of course we realize that much of the so called "wisdom" of the most intelligent, and well-educated among us is "foolishness," and that is how the Bible labels it: "For the wisdom of this world is foolishness in God's sight. As it is written: 'He catches the wise in their craftiness;' and again, 'The Lord knows that the thoughts of the wise are futile' " (1 Corinthians 3:19, 20).

And when Job later responds to God's sublime questioning, he admits he hadn't known God at all! He had just heard of Him, but now in this final experience, Job recognizes the difference between hearsay evidence and experiential evidence of a relationship with God.

Makes a person think, doesn't it? How does our relationship with God measure up? Do we operate on a surface, what-someone-else-said experience—content with secondhand knowledge of God? Or do we have something real that we have experienced with God—leading us to say, as Job said:

> "I know that you can do all things;
>   no purpose of yours can be thwarted.
> You asked, 'Who is this that obscures my plans without
>   knowledge?'
>   Surely I spoke of things I did not understand,
>   things too wonderful for me to know.
> "You said, 'Listen now, and I will speak;
>   I will question you,
>   and you shall answer me.'
> My ears had heard of you
>   but now my eyes have seen you.
> Therefore I despise myself
>   and repent in dust and ashes" (Job 42:2–6).

Now that Job had been exposed to direct contact with God, now that he had an undeniable experience with God, he was able to reevaluate the position he had previously held regarding God.

His statement here reveals a total humility before God. He repents of his words and his attitude, maybe even his thoughts of self-defense under the withering suppositions of his friends. Job reevaluated himself in the context of the new knowledge gained from God's monologue.

It seems that every sincere person who has an encounter with God instantly demonstrates a deep poverty of the soul, or humility, before the Lord. Consider Isaiah, the prophet whose book begins with a sudden bang. He condemns sin right from the start. But then in chapter 6, he has a vision of the throne room of the Almighty. Angels fly around proclaiming the word *holy* in triplicate as a description or name for the Divine.

What an overwhelming experience! One so intense that while having it, Isaiah cried out, "Then said I, Woe is me! for I am undone; because I am a man of unclean lips, and I dwell in the midst of a people of unclean lips: for mine eyes have seen the King, the LORD of hosts" (Isaiah 6:5, KJV).

One source writes, regarding Isaiah's experience, "The cry of the prophet expresses the normal result of man's consciousness of contact with God. So Moses 'hid his face, for he was afraid to look upon God' (Exodus 3:6). So Job 'abhorred himself and repented in dust and ashes' (Job 42:6). So Peter fell down at his Lord's feet, and cried, 'Depart from me, for I am a sinful man, O Lord' (Luke 5:8). Man at such a time feels his nothingness in the presence of the Eternal, his guilt in the presence of the All-holy. No man can see God and live. (Comp. also 1 Samuel 6:20.)"[2]

As Isaiah saw in vision a scene of worship that caused him to proclaim his wickedness, so Job realized his true situation when God dialogued with him. The result was Job repenting and admitting not just his own ignorance but also his utter sinfulness before God.

Despite all that Job experienced, he remained faithful—losing his worldly goods; losing his family all at once; being touched by Satan and thinking it was God; having friends who were not at all helpful; and finally having a visitation of God in the whirlwind.

And through it all, he stayed loyal to God.

Remember, the trial was brought on by Satan for a multiplicity of reasons, including but not limited to: continuing the attack on God, humiliating one of God's faithful, and proving that his faithfulness was purchased—that God had bribed Job by making him wealthy and well-known. But the sudden reversal of Job's fortunes proved God right, as He always is, and Satan a liar, as he always is.

" 'The Lord answered Job out of the whirlwind' (Job 38:1), and revealed to His servant the might of His power. When Job caught a glimpse of his Creator, he abhorred himself and repented in dust and ashes. Then the Lord was able to bless him abundantly and to make his last years the best of his life."[3]

Job came through his extreme test as pure gold. How about us? How would we fare, or how are we faring even now?

Although we would not seek to share in Job's horrendous trials, we can remain faithful—and are kept not by our power, intelligence, or might but by His Spirit.

1. Zuck, "Job," 767.

2. "Isaiah 6," *Ellicott's Commentary for English Readers,* Bible Hub, http://biblehub.com/commentaries/isaiah/6-5.htm

3. White, *Prophets and Kings,* 164.

CHAPTER 12

Job's Redeemer

Has it occurred to you that Job's story also reflects the resolution of the great controversy theme? After all, Job's story winds up pretty good, doesn't it? He has more children, his daughters are fairer than any in the land (Job 42:15), and their names are preserved in sacred history, something that was not done for the seven sons or any of the children mentioned at the beginning of the book.

Job was restored when he prayed for his friends. Job was a praying man. He knew how to seek God. We see his restrained prayer (Job 15:4), purity of prayer (Job 16:17), empty prayer (Job 21:15), profitable prayer (Job 22:27), blessedness of prayer (Job 33:26), interceding prayer (Job 42:8), and emancipating prayer (Job 42:10).[1]

Flash forward across the centuries to the Redeemer Himself. Jesus, we remember, was a praying person, sometimes praying all night and rising in the early hours before sunrise to pray. He often went to isolated or deserted places to pray privately (see Luke 5:16; 6:12; Mark 1:35).

Most notable was Job's intercessory prayer for his friends, the EBZ group. He prayed for his tormentors, even as Jesus prayed for his executioners from the cross. "Jesus said, 'Father, forgive them, for they do not know what they are doing.' And they divided up his clothes by casting lots" (Luke 23:34).

Herewith we have another reflection of Jesus Christ: His capacity and desire to forgive. Where would we be if God wasn't a forgiving Being? In fact, in God's self-revelation to Moses, He described Himself this way: "The LORD, the LORD, the compassionate and gracious God, slow to anger, abounding in love and faithfulness, maintaining love to thousands, and *forgiving wickedness, rebellion and sin.* Yet he does not leave the guilty unpunished; he punishes the children and their children for the sin of the parents to the third and fourth generation" (Exodus 34:6, 7; emphasis added). And remember Christ's instruction regarding forgiveness: "For if you forgive other people when they sin against you, your heavenly Father will also forgive you. But if you do not forgive others their sins, your Father will not forgive your sins" (Matthew 6:14, 15).

Intrinsic to Job's prayer was his attitude of forgiveness; he forgave the ones he prayed for. Thus he fulfilled the requirement for full restoration. But more important than this reflection of Christ's teaching on forgiveness is the reflection of the presence of Christ Himself. Job specifically mentions his Redeemer. How did he know about redemption? We are not sure.

Job was obviously a man of strong hope, and his hope was born of faith; he knew he would see his Redeemer. Check closely the sequence of his statement in Job 19:25, 26. First, he establishes the fact that he *knew* his Redeemer was alive, a reference to the pre-incarnation presence of Jesus the Christ. How did he know? He was "walking" not by sight, but by faith (see 2 Corinthians 5:7). Perhaps Job's faith informed him; the hope for Job was a reality yet not presented to him, but it was as sure as the operation of faith itself.

Is this a partial application of what Paul wrote in Hebrews 11:1? "Now faith is the substance of things hoped for, the evidence of things not seen" (KJV). If so, it was a fact before Paul wrote it. It was operational in Job's day, as it was in the day Adam and Eve were escorted out of the Garden of Eden.

For Job and for every believer before and after him, there is a divine Redeemer. We know His name is Jesus, and at the last day

He will stand up and defend us because He has bought us with His blood (Acts 20:28; Ephesians 1:7; 2:13; Colossians 1:20; 1 Peter 1:18, 19; Revelation 1:5; 5:9).[2]

Job's statement of faith in his Redeemer "represents a significant advance in Job's progress from despair to confidence and hope: 'From the depths of discouragement and despondency Job rose to the heights of implicit trust in the mercy and the saving power of God' (PK 163)."[3]

Next, Job knew that he would die and that his flesh would be consumed. As previously pointed out, Job did not expect to go immediately to heaven when he died. Job did, however, have the expectation that in his flesh he would see God—a direct reference to the resurrection. Job's hope was multifaceted and not simplistic, but complex. His hope in a Redeemer is obviously linked to the Person of Jesus Christ.

Earlier in the book, Job expressed doubts when he asked about God not being a flesh-and-blood-type person. "Have you eyes of flesh? Do you see as man sees? Are your days as the days of man, or your years as a man's years . . . ?" (Job 10:4, 5, ESV).

Job was really expressing the complaint that God could not have understood through experience what he was going through, the physical suffering and mental torment he was enduring. How could God have known experientially what human beings were going through? Did God really relate, understand, and have a clue to what it was like to live in that world of sin and depravity?

In Jesus, we have One who understands because He has experienced it all in an intense manner. Not only is He the Creator God who formed humanity in His image, but He came to become part of the created and to live and die in this world and to be raised again in victory over sin, death, and the grave.

Our God became part of His own creation and made Himself an object of temptation, abuse, scorn, injustice, and execution for us. Truly Paul wrote: "For we do not have a high priest who is unable to sympathize with our weaknesses, but one who in every respect has been tempted as we are, yet without sin. Let us then with confidence draw near to the throne of grace, that we may receive mercy and find grace to help in time of need" (Hebrews 4:15, 16, ESV). Jesus met the devil physically, face to face, was tempted by him—while at His weakest physical and mental point—and overcame the temptation (see Matthew 4:1–11).

The Bible is replete with prophetic statements that are fulfilled in Jesus. Take for example Isaiah 53—where we are told about our Redeemer, who bore all our infirmities and weaknesses and while bearing them was persecuted and executed for us! Or Psalm 22:14:

> I am poured out like water,
>   and all my bones are out of joint.
> My heart has turned to wax;
>   it has melted within me.

Surely, this was fulfilled in our Creator, who is also our Redeemer.

Job's complaint is answered in the birth of Jesus; the Son of God became a true, flesh-and-blood, historical person who came to "seek and to save" the lost. After resisting temptation, He suffered, bled, and died; thus He sympathizes with humanity and is the one Mediator between God and man.

The fact of the incarnational ministry of Jesus is not something we can prove empirically. However, we accept the Bible as the Word of God about *the* Word who *is* God. As one preacher put it, if we try to understand how God became man without ceasing to be God, we may lose our minds; if we don't accept the fact by faith, we may lose our souls!

The fact that Jesus came and lived a life of victory is proof that we can do it too. There is no biblical evidence that the divinity of Jesus gave Him any advantage in the battle against sin, Satan, and evil. He lived fully as a man without depending on the power of His divine nature.

Remember, Jesus suffered violence to secure our souls. He paid the purchase price of the rarest commodity that ever existed: His righteous blood.

It stands to reason that if humanity could have been saved and made righteous simply by obeying the law, it would have happened. However, Scripture clarifies the question by presenting the futility of the dependency of humans on their so-called obedience to satisfy the claims of our Holy God (see Galatians 2:16, 3:11). "He who is trying to become holy by his own works in keeping the law, is attempting an impossibility."[4]

Our law keeping is not enough, because our very natures are "fallen." Selfishness, which leads to sin, taints us to the core. Not so with Jesus, the only perfect Man. His obedience alone can atone for sin. Not only is He our atonement, our purchase price itself, He is our Exemplar, our Example in all things pertaining to righteousness.

The only way to fully understand the book of Job is through the lens of Calvary. The sacrificial death of Jesus gives meaning to what Job and every other sufferer has ever or will ever experience.

Yesterday I was reminded:

Hanging upon the cross, Christ was the gospel. Now we have a message, "Behold the Lamb of God, which taketh away the sins of the world." Will not our church members keep their eyes fixed on a crucified and risen Saviour, in whom their hopes of eternal life are centered? This is our message, our argument, our doctrine, our warning to the impenitent, our encouragement for the sorrowing, the hope for every believer. If we can awaken an interest in men's minds that will cause them to fix their eyes on Christ, we may step aside, and ask them only to continue to fix their eyes upon the Lamb of God. They thus receive their lesson. Whosoever will come after Me, let him deny himself, and take up his cross, and follow Me. He whose eyes are fixed on Jesus will leave all. He will die to selfishness. He will believe in all the Word of God, which is so gloriously and wonderfully exalted in Christ.[5]

In Job, we better understand the sacrifice of God in Christ

Jesus. He is the one who went to the cross suffering a much deeper trial than Job could know. Throughout our study of Job, we think of his innocence and the unfairness that he experienced. Think of the unfairness of Jesus' coming to this earth and living a life of obscurity leading up to His ministry. Think of His sacrificing the worship of the angels and the limits His flesh put upon Him. Think of the scorn heaped upon Him all His life as many neighbors viewed Him as Mary's illegitimate child. He was truly innocent of all the charges brought against Him, but He carried the weight of every human sin to Calvary.

Both Job and Jesus experienced the unwarranted wrath of the enemy, Satan. By the sufferings of Christ, the perfect sacrifice of the only perfect Man—his death, burial, and resurrection—Satan was "unmasked" and dethroned.

Satan is consistently portrayed in the Bible as the accuser of the brethren and God; he is the adversary who appears among the sons of God (Job 1:6; 2:1), not as one to worship, but only to criticize. He is indifferent to the claims of the Divine and does not delight in the works of God. He is an unbeliever in the extreme representation of all doubters. He knows but refuses to believe as an expression of faith in God. And he is consistently cruel, taking his cruelty to the apex in the execution—the assassination—of Jesus Christ.[6]

Please forgive this long quotation from the pen of inspiration. I cannot state it any better, so I have decided to close this chapter with the following words:

> Through Jesus, God's mercy was manifested to men; but mercy does not set aside justice. The law reveals the attributes of God's character, and not a jot or tittle of it could be changed to meet man in his fallen condition. God did not change His law, but He sacrificed Himself, in Christ, for man's redemption. "God was in Christ, reconciling the world unto Himself" (2 Corinthians 5:19).
>
> The law requires righteousness,—a righteous life, a perfect character; and this man has not to give. He cannot meet the claims of God's holy law. But Christ, coming

to the earth as man, lived a holy life, and developed a perfect character. These He offers as a free gift to all who will receive them. His life stands for the life of men. Thus they have remission of sins that are past, through the forbearance of God. More than this, Christ imbues men with the attributes of God. He builds up the human character after the similitude of the divine character, a goodly fabric of spiritual strength and beauty. Thus the very righteousness of the law is fulfilled in the believer in Christ. God can "be just, and the justifier of him which believeth in Jesus" (Romans 3:26).[7]

What a God we serve!

1. Herbert Lockyer, *All the Men of the Bible* (Grand Rapids, Mich.: Zondervan, 1958), 192.

2. Alden, "Job," 207.

3. Nichol, *The Seventh-day Adventist Bible Commentary,* vol. 3, 549.

4. White, *Steps to Christ,* 60.

5. Ellen G. White, MR no. 1507, written April 9, 1898, *Manuscript Releases,* vol. 21 (Silver Spring, Md.: Ellen G. White Estate, 1993).

6. See Robertson W. Nicoll, ed., *The Sermon Outline Bible: Genesis to 2 Samuel,* Preachers Homiletic Library, vol. 1, (Grand Rapids, Mich.: Baker Book House, 1979), 179.

7. Ellen G. White, *The Desire of Ages* (Mountain View, Calif.: Pacific Press, 1898), 762.

CHAPTER 13

The Character of Job

In our study of Job, we are brought full circle to reexamine an intrinsic part of the book: Job's character.

Let's look up the word *character* in the dictionary, just to arrive at a common understanding of what the word means.

One dictionary defines *character* as "the mental and moral qualities distinctive to an individual." Another says it is "the complex of mental and ethical traits marking a person." In still another dictionary, *character* is said to be "the stable and distinctive qualities built into an individual's life which determine his or her response regardless of circumstances." Abraham Lincoln said, "Reputation is the shadow. Character is the tree."[1]

These mental and moral qualities are revealed in the life as it is lived daily in the contextual situation we find ourselves.

From the very beginning of the book of Job, the main character is noted to be of sterling character: "In the land of Uz there lived a man whose name was Job. This man was blameless and upright; he feared God and shunned evil" (Job 1:1). His entire experience is summed up in just a few words—twenty-five to be exact—in the New International Version. In fact, we can say from our study thus far that nothing we have read in the book about this man has changed, even though he was severely tested and tried by the enemy of our souls, Satan.

It is clear due to the pronouncement and articulation of God Himself that it is possible—despite all hellish opposition—to live a life pleasing to God at any time, in any society, under any political system.

The writer of the book evaluates Job with four notable character traits in Job 1:1, and this evaluation is repeated by God Himself to Satan in verse 8. These characteristics are significant, worthy of our exploration for the sake of emulation and inculcation in our own lives.

"In the land of Uz there lived a man whose name was Job. This man was blameless[2] and upright; he feared God and shunned evil" (verse 1).

Job was "blameless." Today, when we read this through our twenty-first-century filter, we may equate being blameless with "perfection." And we immediately think, *How can this happen?* We need to be informed by the original language of the writer. In our exposition and interpretation of the Bible, we often forget that the Bible writers used languages much different from ours. Often, when transliterated or translated, the full meaning of the words fails to come across to our modern minds the way the writer intended for them to be understood in his own time, culture, and circumstance.

Taken as a whole, the Bible describes humanity in its "fallen-ness" as being quite "blamable," to coin a phrase. Consider for instance the New Testament witness of Romans 3:10: "As it is written: 'There is no one righteous, not even one;' " and 3:23: "for all have sinned and fall short of the glory of God." The consistent witness of Scripture is that in the aftermath of the fall of humanity in the Garden of Eden, all of us are sinful, or full of sin.

Jeremiah 17:9 is accurate in stating, "The heart is deceitful above all things, and desperately wicked: who can know it?" (KJV). In all honesty, Jeremiah reminds us that we really don't even know the lengths of the depravity of our inmost being. God tells us in Scripture of His divine assessment of all humanity, and that is why He calls us to repentance, revival, and reformation, or transformation (see Isaiah 1:18).

Likewise, God alone is absolutely perfect. Jesus is the only person who lived a perfect life. Period.

Of course, there have been several notable and good people, and reference is made of them in Scripture. Think of Enoch, who walked so closely to God that God "took" him home to heaven (See Genesis 5:24 and Hebrews 11:5.) Or what about Elijah the Tishbite, who served God as a prophet and was taken to heaven in a chariot of fire? (See 2 Kings 2:11, 12.) And, God declared that Noah, Daniel, and Job had achieved a level of righteousness. "Even if Noah, Daniel, and Job were there, their righteousness would save no one but themselves, says the Sovereign LORD" (Ezekiel 14:14, NLT).

While Job is accounted righteous by the Lord, he, like us, was not perfect.

David testifies to the fallen nature of humanity. Under inspiration of the Holy Spirit, he proclaimed his "fallen-ness" from birth: "Surely I was sinful at birth, sinful from the time my mother conceived me" (Psalm 51:5). That is why Jesus said: "Very truly I tell you, no one can enter the kingdom of God unless they are born of water and the Spirit" (John 3:5). Jesus expressed an eternal truth with this statement.

However, while it is true that we are fallen, it is also true that we can live blamelessly before God and our neighbors.

So what is this "blameless" state that Job achieved? A true understanding of the Hebrew word translated here as "blameless," *tam,* will help in our understanding. The word *tam* really means, "mature." *Tam* (תֹּם), the word translated "perfect," is consistently interpreted to mean "complete, entire, not wanting in any respect." Not absolute *sinlessness*, or perfection, but blameless in a *relative* sense. Here the word *tam* means that a person has reached the degree of maturity or completeness God expects at any given moment in time. Like a snapshot in time, God said that at the time of the statement, Job had demonstrated a level of growth, development, and processing in life that God, our true Judge,[3] alone could determine.

Let me illustrate. A newborn baby girl may be perfect as a baby but certainly not in comparison to a full-grown woman. She is progressing, growing, developing. At any given time under the examination of a pediatrician, a baby can be pronounced "perfect." What the doctor means is that the particular infant has developed as expected. She is "mature" or maturing. The physician cannot find anything wrong with the baby's progress or development.

As God looks at us at any time, He expects us to be blameless; without cause for blame, because we are operating in our lives at the level He expects of us at the time He is looking at us.

It is Jesus—through the indwelling of the Holy Spirit—who directs our spiritual development and growth. It is clear to me that God judged Job as blameless because God is quoted as saying such to the enemy, Satan.

We may wonder, how did Job come to the knowledge of righteousness, or how did he come to possess the expectations of God when they are not stated in the book bearing Job's name? While it is true that there is no internal information to warrant arrival at this conclusion, logic leads us by inductive reasoning to the assumption that somewhere at some time, he was exposed to truth. At some point in his life, things of eternal consequences were revealed to Job.

The Bible teaches that Job was also "upright." The Hebrew word וישר, *vejashar,* is most often translated as "right," "exact," and "regular." Job was right and exact in all his dealings with men; he was a person of unblamable conversation.[4] Neither God nor his human contacts had anything to blame Job about; amazing—though it seems impossible. Although we may be unable to name any of our friends or business associates or leaders in our society who have reached this high estate, it is not impossible with God. Nothing that God commands is impossible. In fact, Jesus clearly taught that *all* things are possible to him who believes (Mark 10:27). And it is the expectation that all who enter into eternity with God will have achieved this state of blamelessness and uprightness.

The natural question that arises may be, "how?" How does a man or woman living in the twenty-first century, with all of its conspicuous, demanding, and prevailing sin, grow into a position that they are known by other people and pronounced by God Himself to be "blameless" and "upright"? My contention is that all God-lauding characteristics are attainable only by the operation of God working in us. Living in His grace, learning to trust Him daily, and actually depending on Him result in His shaping us into blameless, upright, God-fearing and evil-avoiding people. And this is doable in the twenty-first century.

By now you may be wondering whether I think I have achieved this state. I can only say like Paul said, in Philippians 3:13, 14, "Brethren, I count not myself to have apprehended: but this one thing I do, forgetting those things which are behind, and reaching forth unto those things which are before, I press toward the mark for the prize of the high calling of God in Christ Jesus" (KJV). Like every other child of God, it is my desire to always compliantly press toward the mark. And I can say, please pray for me that I may one day be blameless, upright, God-fearing, and evil-avoiding. I believe it was the late Elder C. T. Richards, professor of religion and theology during my freshman year at Oakwood College (now University), who paraphrased John Newton while preaching one Sabbath, saying, "I am not what I want to be, I am not what I am going to be, but I thank God that I am not what I used to be."

The marvelous, loving God accepts us all along the path we walk to becoming what He has called us to be. Trusting God and obeying Him, our lives are covered by His grace, and His grace is more than unmerited favor. Yes, grace is unearned and undeserved, but it was never given by God to cover or hide sin. Grace is the power that fuels our desire and ability to humbly live the life God calls us to and of which Job stands as an excellent, though ancient, example of.

Someone has said, "Reputation is what others think of you; character is what you are." John Wooden (October 14, 1910–June 4, 2010) was an American basketball player and coach. Nicknamed the "Wizard of Westwood," as head coach at UCLA (University of California, Los Angeles) he won ten NCAA (National Collegiate Athletic Association) national championships in a twelve-year period, including an unprecedented seven in a row.

He said, "The true test of a man's character is what he does when no one is watching." A coworker of mine once told me that what other people say about me (reputation) wasn't my business. What God thought of me was (is).

While the aforementioned may be true, the Bible does record, as Job himself relates, what others thought of him before his trial. He was a successful businessman, respected by young and honored by old. He was welcomed at the city gates, a place normally associated with the seat of the learned and revered in the location. The populace acknowledged Job as a leader—and perhaps the most prominent of leaders of his time and place, as noted in the words, "He was the greatest man among all the people of the East" (Job 1:3). To say he was "highly respected" is probably an understatement. And yet all people, not just the religious or spiritual folks but even those who are not religious, value respect. Gangs in today's societies fight over a notion, misguided though it may be in perception and actuality, of the lack of respect or disrespect.

Job was valued, respected, and honored because he treated even the lowliest of his day with regard and respect. He delivered the poor and helped the fatherless. He was not just a saint on Saturdays, but he made a difference in the lives of those around him every day.

God valued Job's activity because in reality, Job was living out what Jesus taught in the parable of the sheep and goats. Remember the story that talks about the last judgment? Jesus said that those who feed the hungry, visit the sick and incarcerated, and clothe the naked are really ministering to Him.

Job apparently had lived a life of true religion summarized in James 1:27: "Pure religion and undefiled before God and the Father is this, To visit the fatherless and widows in their affliction, and to keep himself unspotted from the world" (KJV). But that is not all. Job did not covet or look lustfully on a woman; he had purity of thought, word, and deed. Thus, he maintained integrity before God.

Also, Job showed no partiality. He treated everyone the same. No ethnocentricity or racism resided within him, which was probably very unusual in his day. Job even treated his slaves as people, not as possessions. He respected all human life as though it had equal value.

Have you ever witnessed the building of a skyscraper? A tall, multistory building that seems to penetrate the clouds? The kind that makes you lean back in an attempt to see how high it rises? It is my understanding that the higher they are built, the deeper and more solid the foundation needs to be. This is an apt description of what it takes to "rise" in character with God—a deep and true spirituality is needed in order to rise in the expectations of God. Jesus emphasized this when he talked about building on the rock rather than on the sinking sand (see Matthew 7:27, 28).

I believe that Job had a real experience with God that could not be shaken, one that glorified God in his good works as specified in Job 31. In fact, it occurs to me that Job 31 could be the male-descriptive counterpart to Proverbs 31:10–31, where the portrayal of the virtuous wife is found.

What does God think of us? What is our reputation with God, and more importantly, what is our character evaluation before Him?

Doing good—being good—in Christ, is the goal of the Christian. According to Scripture, despite the trials, tribulations, and temptation Job endured, he obviously made the grade.

---

1. Larry Roach, "What Did Abraham Lincoln Say About Character?" *What Is Character?* (blog), http://www.character-training.com/blog/.

2. While the King James Version uses the word *perfect,* the NIV, NLT, NASB, ESV and several others use the word *blameless,* which I have chosen to use also.

3. 1 Samuel 24:15; Genesis 18:25.

4. "Job 1," *Benson Commentary,* Bible Hub, http://biblehub.com/commentaries /benson/job/1.htm.

CHAPTER

Some Lessons From Job

As we conclude our study on the book of Job, there are several key points that speak to us across the centuries that are relevant to our life situation.

Foremost among them is the fact that it is possible to live a blameless and upright life before God. After all, Job was called blameless, upright, God-fearing, and an avoider of evil at least three times in the opening chapters of the book. (Job 1:1; 1:8; 2:3). And in the second and third recitations of Job's character attributes, God Himself is quoted. We understand that Job's blamelessness meant *maturity*, and not absolute perfection.

Job was obedient to God; but his obedience, as well as ours, is tainted. We obey, knowing that Jesus, our Redeemer, is the true source of our obedience and that His merits stand for us before God.

We also see that Job was punctilious in his religious responsibility. He offered sacrifices for his children, and it is most likely, though not stated, that he offered sacrifices for himself and his wife.

Job reminds us of the high spiritual calling of godly parenthood, for becoming a parent is a lifelong calling to intercessory prayer. Parents must pray for their children; after all, having children is a lifelong commitment. Yes, we raise them to the age of accountability and "launch" them into life through education and training. However, we are never released from influencing them for God. Job also prayed for his well-meaning but misguided friends, and God associated Job's prayers for them with his complete recovery. We need to pray as never before as the end of time draws near.

We realize that the great controversy theme is resident in the book of Job, for we have seen the presence of evil displayed in the attack of the devil on this good man. It reminds us that bad things happen to good people—for which there is not always a cause and effect; the reason why things happen the way they do often escapes our reason and knowledge. Trouble such as disease and automobile accidents may seem to come from nowhere or from "randomness," but the story of Job makes it clear that evil is present in the world because of Satan. He and the other fallen angels continue to attack and plague the lives of all humanity but especially the faithful, like Job.

What is clear from the narrative is not only that Job was attacked but also how he responded to it. While we cannot control what the devil sends to us and how he attacks us, we can be sure of certain things: God is aware, and He controls the devil's activities (Job 1:12; 2:6). Satan and his agents cannot do more than God allows them to do under their usurped rulership of planet Earth.

We determine how we respond to the evil that befalls us. When Job was under attack, he worshiped God. We must always praise God. In good times and bad, whether happy or sad, the true child of God will remember to assume the position of a worshiper. Job refused to blame God while he was attacked (Job 1:21, 22).

Another lesson that we derive from our study is that friends are essential to life. Job's three friends showed up to support him, and the best thing they did was sit silently with him while he mourned. Jesus had twelve, and among the twelve his closest were Peter, John, and James.

We need the support of Christian friends and family members. We are not islands to ourselves, cut off from other people, and we cannot think that we can make it as "rugged individuals" to the kingdom of God, to heaven. No, if we are going to succeed in any endeavor, we need support. One thing that we learn from sporting events is that one player cannot win the game. It takes a team. Jesus is the Captain, and we all must follow His lead; by leaning on each other and following His lead, we can all win.

No one is immune to the attacks of Satan, he attacks all of us; but God protects His own. When Satan said that God had placed a hedge around Job, he told the truth, for once, even though he was misusing the truth to secure his own goal—the attack on an innocent man. If we realize that what is true in the natural realm is also true in the spiritual, we can understand that it is only natural for a person to protect his or her property. When we consign ourselves to the rulership of Jesus, He marks us as His for the entire universe to see.

In fact, Revelation 7:1–4 makes plain that the great time of trouble will not start until God's servants are sealed. A seal accomplishes many things, and one is a sign of ownership. God has the right to protect those whom He owns. Luke records another statement of God's protective care over us even when we are under the glaring gaze of Satan:

"And the Lord said, Simon, Simon, behold, Satan hath desired to have you, that he may sift you as wheat: But I have prayed for thee, that thy faith fail not: and when thou art converted, strengthen thy brethren" (Luke 22:31, 32, KJV).

Jesus prayed for Simon Peter as a source of protection for him, to keep him from being "sifted" as wheat. Jesus wanted to protect His erring disciple, even before the disciple could understand the import of the prophetic statements Jesus was making.

Interestingly enough, the book of Job never states that Job received any direct answers to his questions. Instead, God revealed himself to Job through the questions He asked. It is almost as if God was saying, "I am the Creator. I have the world and everything in it under control. I've got you, too. Trust Me." God drew Job's attention to Himself. We must look away from self and look to God through Jesus.

We may not know why we undergo trials, tribulations, and

troubles. They may be God's methodology for maturing us in Him. But we will reap the reward of the faithful, as Job certainly will, based on the internal testimony of the book. Thus, Job's end was better than his beginning. He had more children and more cattle, and he died a man full of days.

We are reminded, "As you know, we count as blessed those who have persevered. You have heard of Job's perseverance and have seen what the Lord finally brought about. The Lord is full of compassion and mercy" (James 5:11). Clearly, Job is counted as a blessed man because he persevered through his troubles. He never gave up hope. He always kept his faith.

The *Seventh-day Adventist Bible Commentary* makes this statement based on James 5:11: "Constant faithfulness amid the problems of life . . . reveals an undivided loyalty to God and becomes a requisite for eternal life. . . . When church members are called to endure hardships, they can claim the same blessings."[1]

I don't think any of us will be called on by God to experience what Job went through—the loss of all possessions; the loss of all children, in a freakish accident; the contraction of a debilitating, incurable disease—surrounded by friends who tell us that, in essence, we are getting what we deserve from God. But even if we are, the faith that God gives us in Him can keep us faithful and loyal to Him through it all.

Andraé Crouch, the late gospel musician, wrote more than 300 songs. One of his most well-known songs, "Through It All," has these words:

> I thank God for the mountains,
> And I thank Him for the valleys,
> I thank Him for the storms
> He's brought me through;
> Cause if I'd never had a problem
> I wouldn't know that He could solve them,
> I'd never know what faith in God could do.
>
> Through it all, through it all,
> I've learned to trust in Jesus,

Some Lessons From Job

I've learned to trust in God;
Through it all, through it all,
I've learned to depend upon His Word.[2]

Christians learn to walk by faith and not by sight. We are called to humility, called to be humble with the Lord. As Micah 6:8 says, in its triple requirement:

> "He has shown you, O mortal, what is good.
> And what does the LORD require of you?
> To act justly and to love mercy
> and to walk humbly with your God."

Nothing is a better antidote for this than looking beyond the present to the future instead. Job teaches us that there is so much activity around us that we do not see. While we focus on the unseen activity of the enemy, we also believe that holy angels of God are involved in the unseen activity all around us.

Do you ask for God's protection when you enter your vehicle and steer it onto the highways and freeways of the city you live in? You are requesting the power of God, unseen but real and delivered by angels to escort you on your way. And God answers these prayers as it is befitting His plan for the world.

While evil is ever present in the world—just view one of the news or media outlets available or streamed into our homes via the Internet—God is present now just as He was with Job. Whether it is natural evil from natural disasters or moral evil from dictators and despots, it all started with Satan.

Our study makes plain that Job was good, and because of his goodness (not quite perfection), Satan asked to test and try him. His hope was that Job would suffer a failure of faith, that he would "curse God and die." Had Job done that, Satan would have won a critical battle in the great controversy and "proved" God unethical.

Remember that Satan was cast out of heaven (Revelation 12:9) after his failed coup; still angry that he lost in heaven, he continues his warfare against God by attacking earthlings. Ultimately

Satan wants to be worshiped (see Matthew 4:8–10); he sows evil in our hearts and minds as an enemy would plant weeds in a farmer's crops (see Matthew 13:39). That is why Jesus makes a clear distinction between Himself and the devil in John 10:10. Realizing all this and more about the battle between good and evil, between God and the devil, should we not be compassionate and graceful when our friends and family suffer unexplainable suffering?

Someone said, "There but for the grace of God, go I." Even if a person were guilty of some great sin, we should strive to be like Jesus, who while pointing out sin did so with grace and forgiveness.

Is there any comparison between Jesus and Job? There are several; the parallels are easy to see. Other than being a witness to what personal faith and perseverance could produce, Job, while not perfect, suffered without a cause beyond himself. Jesus, who was and is perfect, suffered for the sins of all humanity. While no wrong was recorded on the behalf of either Jesus or Job, they were both attacked by Satan and falsely accused. Both endured suffering that was more than intense. But the suffering caused by sin was not limited to Job or Jesus.

> Few give thought to the suffering that sin has caused our Creator. All heaven suffered in Christ's agony; but that suffering did not begin or end with His manifestation in humanity. The cross is a revelation to our dull senses of the pain that, from its very inception, sin has brought to the heart of God. Every departure from the right, every deed of cruelty, every failure of humanity to reach His ideal, brings grief to Him. When there came upon Israel the calamities that were the sure result of separation from God,—subjugation by their enemies, cruelty, and death,—it is said that "His soul was grieved for the misery of Israel." "In all their affliction He was afflicted: . . . and He bare them, and carried them all the days of old." (Judges 10:16; Isaiah 63:9).[3]

One day, all sin and suffering will be over. We will rejoice in that day as described by the same author in her great work, *The Great Controversy*: "The great controversy is ended. Sin and sinners are no more. The entire universe is clean. One pulse of harmony and gladness beats through the vast creation. From Him who created all, flow life and light and gladness, throughout the realms of illimitable space. From the minutest atom to the greatest world, all things, animate and inanimate, in their unshadowed beauty and perfect joy, declare that God is love."[4]

We long for the day when that will be a reality.

---

1. Nichol, *The Seventh-day Adventist Bible Commentary,* vol. 7, 539.

2. Andraé Crouch, "Through It All," © 1971 Manna Music, Inc.

3. White, *Education,* 263.

4. Ellen G. White, *The Great Controversy* (Nampa, Idaho: Pacific Press®, 1999), 678.

Notes

Notes

Notes

Notes

Notes

Notes

Notes

Notes

Notes

Notes

Notes